PLAIN & FANCY

PLAIN & FANCY

Country Quilts of the Pennsylvania-Germans

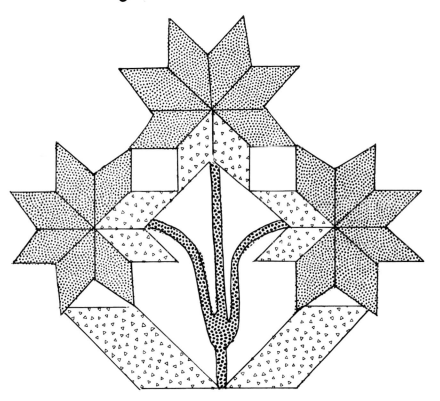

Anita Schorsch

A Sterling/Main Street Book
Sterling Publishing Co., Inc.   New York

Library of Congress Cataloging-in-Publication Data

Schorsch, Anita.
    Plain & fancy : country quilts of the Pennsylvania-Germans / Anita
Schorsch,
        p. cm.
    "A Sterling/Main Street book."
    Includes bibliographical references and index.
    ISBN 0-8069-7432-X
    1. Quilts—Pennsylvania—Pennsylvania Dutch Country—Themes,
motives. I. Title. II. Title: Plain and fancy.
NK9112.S34   1991
746.9′7′088310748—dc20   90-23692
                                          CIP

Designed by John Murphy

10 9 8 7 6 5 4 3 2 1

A Sterling/Main Street Book

© 1992 by Anita Schorsch
Published by Sterling Publishing Company, Inc.
387 Park Avenue South, New York, N.Y. 10016.
Distributed in Canada by Sterling Publishing
% Canadian Manda Group, P.O. Box 920, Station U
Toronto, Ontario, Canada M8Z 5P9.
Distributed in Great Britain and Europe by Cassell PLC
Villiers House, 41/47 Strand, London WC2N 5JE, England.
Distributed in Australia by Capricorn Ltd.
P.O. Box 665, Lane Cove, NSW 2066.
Manufactured in the United States of America

Sterling ISBN 0-8069-7432-X

Contents

Preface

IT IS A MISTAKE to think we can do anything valuable alone. Writing a book, even one on as delightful a subject as quilts, requires the authority of centuries of objects and texts as well as the relevancy of craftspeople and researchers of today. Individualists of the modern era still feel a communal spirit with their past and remember and respond to thoughts and images unself-consciously influencing their taste, their eyes, and their hands.

I owe a debt to many scholars, craftspeople, and theologians of the past for the material in this book. My bibliography, at the end of the book, acknowledges these "oldest" of debts. Here, at the beginning of the book, I would like to acknowledge the many scholars, craftspeople, and theologians of the present who encouraged me to see art as an aspect of religion and to identify these religious impulses with what is currently called "gender culture."

Inspiration for the direction of this book has come from two men who in their own work have observed connections between religion and material culture, between literary text and visual design, between the word and the image. Dr. James I. McCord, President Emeritus, Princeton Theological Seminary, and Chancellor Emeritus, Center of Theological Inquiry, and Hugh T. Kerr, Benjamin B. Warfield Professor Emeritus of Systematic Theology, Princeton Theological Seminary, and Senior Editor of *Theology Today*, supported and encouraged my belief in the spirituality of human artistic endeavor. Hugh Kerr generously reviewed and criticized my text as did Horton M. Davies, Henry Putnam Professor of Religion, Princeton University, and visiting lecturer in Liturgics, Princeton Theological Seminary; Diogenes Allen, Stuart Professor of Philosophy, Princeton Theological Sminary; and Randall Miller, Professor of History, Saint Joseph's University, and Editor-in-Chief, *Pennsylvania Magazine of History and Biography*. Specific insight into the Lutheran and Mennonite traditions has been graciously offered by the Reverends John Goerss and John Ruth.

I am indebted to Charles F. Hummel, Deputy Director of Collections, Henry Francis du Pont Winterthur Museum, and Beatrice Garvan, former Curator of American Decorative Arts, Philadelphia Museum of Art, who shared with me their expert analyses of the roots of the Pennsylvania-German aesthetic tradition as it existed in Germany. Patricia Herr, quilt scholar, and Joel Alderfer of the Mennonite Heritage Center, generously gave time, information, and quilts to this study. The research of Jeanette Lasansky, Director, Oral Traditions Project, Union County, contributed extensive primary source documentation to balance the theoretical positions I have been exploring. Painstakingly, her staff collected remembered data from quilting families in Middle Pennsylvania. Dr. David J. Rempel Smucker, Genealogist, Lancaster Mennonite Historical Society, helpfully identified the history of local families and put me in touch with such families as those of Dorothy Nissley of "eagle quilt" fame. The scholarship of Peter C. Erb of the Schwenkfelder Library and Wilfrid Laurier University recalled once again for me the power of medieval iconography in the lives of the Pennsylvania-German sectarians.

Carol E. Faill, Administrator of College Collections, Franklin and Marshall College, provided a large number of quilts for photographing which have never been included in any previous publication. Other museum directors and staff members have added objects and interpretations which I gratefully considered in developing the body of my book. Among those whom I wish to thank are Margaret Vincent, Curator of Textiles, Allentown Art Museum; Lucy R. Eldridge, Registrar, Mercer Museum; Mary Jane Lederach Hershey, Mennonite Heritage Center; Barbara Luck, Director, Abby Aldrich Folk Art Museum, Colonial Williamsburg; Harold Yoder, Director, Anne W. Goda, Curator, and Barbara Gill, Librarian, Historical Society of Berks County; Barbara K. Abrams, Curator, Germantown Historical Society; Ann Barton Brown, Associate Director, Margaret Bleecker Blades and Sara Wilson, Curators, Chester County HIstorical Society; Patricia J. Keller-Conner, Director, and Susan Messimer, Curator, Heritage Center of Lancaster; Gerald Bastoni, Director, Kemerer Museum of Decorative Arts; Beth Pierce, Curator, Moravian Museum; Gail M, Getz, Curator, The State Museum of Pennsylvania; Claire Conway, Schwenkfelder Library; Patrick Holtz, Director, and Wade Lawrence, Curator, Historical Society of York County.

I am grateful for the skillful assistance of Nancy Roan and Holly Green, and for the generosity of the following collectors who allowed their quilts to be photographed for this book—Patricia Herr, Amy Finkel, Nancy Roan, Holly Green, Irvin and Marilyn Schorsch, John and Joan Schorsch, Victor and Joan Johnson, Stephen and Nancy Palmer, Jr., Howard Schanely, Joseph and Joan Reese, Jeffrey and Laura Kahn—as well as the staffs of the many museum collections already mentioned. The partners of Israel Sack, Inc., and the staff of the Rare Book division of the Philadelphia Free Library graciously allowed art objects relating to quilt patterns to be photographed.

The following photographers have made this book possible: Ken White, Hackettstown, New Jersey; George Fistrovich, Winterthur Museum; Joan Broderick, Philadelphia; and John W. Munro, Harleysville, Pennsylvania. My three daughters—Bonnie, Marilyn, and Shelley— were immeasurably halpful in the initial cataloging of the quilts, and Doris Dinger was particularly diligent in making the text legible. But, most important, have been the contributions of Irvin G. Schorsch, Jr., my husband, who patiently and cheerfully lived through this book with me.

1. Quilt Patterns as Part of History

IT IS A COMMONPLACE NOWADAYS to assume that a Pennsylvania-German quilt is a piece of American history, art in its own right, the result of women friends at work, and a product of the American countryside. It is less commonly realized that a Pennsylvania-German quilt is part of ancient history and, in that context, a reflection of spiritual life. Not that quilts, or more particularly quilting designs, suggest a rational system of theology—but, just the same, they represent the spirit in a display of permissable and pious designs passed down by custom and culture.

1.1. Detail, pieced and appliquéd signature quilt made for Mrs.. Anora Richards, wife of Pastor John William Richards of St. Michael's Lutheran Church, Germantown. Patch, dated August 20, 1843, made by Mary Ann Tungkurth. An open Bible, with the inscription "Search the Scriptures," is drawn in ink. Lutherans and other churchly Pennsylvania Germans were more willing than the radical Protestant sects to inscribe their artwork with biblical texts. Collection of Germantown Historical Society; photograph by Ken White.

People of German churches and sects believed that art and religion, like work and play, were everyday experiences. Choosing acceptable piecing and stitching designs would have been as much a spiritual decision as adopting appropriate behavorial codes or selecting a stable minister. Guidance in decision–making was considered divine and inspired. To churchly people—the Lutherans and Reformed—inspiration came through reading the Bible.[1] Luther never wanted culture to overrun Christian character. As one quilter inscribed on her quilt, "Search the Scriptures" (figure 1.1). To the sects or "House Germans"—Mennonites and groups derived from them—inspiration was a more internal and immediate experience than reading.[2] And it was actually this choice of looking at life, and at quilts, through the heart or the head which made people say that the Pennsylvania Germans were either "plain or fancy."

Religion played its part in the history of the quilt despite the old and still new fear of tying religion too close to human or humane activity. Old tensions over who might be in control over church and state connections still reside in the American and the Protestant psyches. But despite the initial break between religious and civil institutions in the 1500s when Luther led the Reformation against the medieval church, art—churchly and domestic, public and private, formal and folk continues to speak to the mystic in everyone, continues to reach towards the abstraction we call mind or the sentiment we call heart.[3] Through the logic or poetry of symbols, art in words, paint, clay, and fabric stimulates our awareness of infinity, of what is beyond human limits. In this general sense aesthetics is an infinite—that is, religious—experience. But, as one Philadelphia Lutheran quilter cautioned believers, "A finite mind can never comprehend the Infinite One" (figure 1.2).

For the pietistic woman of Pennsylvania the quilt was a particular aspect of the evangelical nineteenth century, one way she had of using the natural and astronomical religious symbols of her heritage and, like the minister, stretching herself through symbols towards the impossible—human perfection (figure 1.3). The process of quilting added to a woman's exemplary nature and to the possibility she would be remembered for her commitment. Quilts were often explicit memorials. "When years shall have fled/Ah how rapid they fly!/'Tis the dearest that die;/This boon may restore;/On these blocks thou canst trace/by memory's sweet lore;/Ev'ry friend—ev'ry face" (figure 1.4). And, with the increase of mysticism among Germans and Americans in the romantic nineteenth century, it was easy for women to see their designs as spiritual statements. Like the Lutheran quilter who included a bird she called Zion and verses inspired by Isaiah, women did indeed see themselves as wives working for their Lord—-the "troubadour of divine love."[4]

This book attempts to explore some of the original meanings behind the symbols used and understood by Pennsylvania-German quilters. As in most tasks they performed and most objects they created, the quilters in early America used a medieval "message system" in the conservative task of supporting and protecting what was most important to them—

1.2. Detail, pieced and appliquéd signature quilt made for Mrs. Anora Richards, wife of Pastor John William Richards of St. Michael's Lutheran Church, Germantown. Patch, dated 1844, made by Sara Roop of Roxborough. Collection of Germantown Historical Society; photograph by Ken White.

1.3. Detail, pieced and appliquéd quilt, probably Lutheran, dated 1881, Lebanon County. Made by Edna E. Meyer. For another quilt bearing the same signature and date, see figure 3.21. Collection of Dr. and Mrs. Donald M. Herr; photograph by Ken White.

1.4. Detail, pieced and appliquéd signature quilt made for Mrs. Anora Richards. Patch dated November, 1843. Collection of Germantown Historical Society; photograph by Ken White.

1.3

1.4

1.5. Compass design in a fifteenth-century Yemenese Pentateuch, now in the British Museum. Throughout history the circle has been identified with celestial bodies, with untameable power, with God. The symbol of the circle appealed to both churchly and sectarian Pennsylvania-German craftspeople.

1.6. Drawings from Soulier de Chelette and Deonna. The circle was a sign both of reason and of mysticism. Like other celestial designs, it appealed to traditional quilters and also to the abstract tastes of the Amish.

1.7. Mariner's Compass, pieced quilt, probably Lutheran or Reformed, c. 1860, locale unknown. Maker unknown. 83" x 88". "Keep within the Compass" was another familiar reference and image for traditional German and English people in eighteenth-century America, meaning, of course, that they should behave themselves on earth so that they might live the next life in heaven. Collection of Robert L. Schaeffer, Jr., in Permanent Collection, Franklin and Marshall College; photograph by Ken White.

"the good life." According to contemporary scholars, Pennsylvania-Germans emigrated to America mainly from the weaving centers of Germany and Switzerland and as such were part of an already established group of artisans using the vocabulary of stars and circles which they shared in all ages and from many places around the world

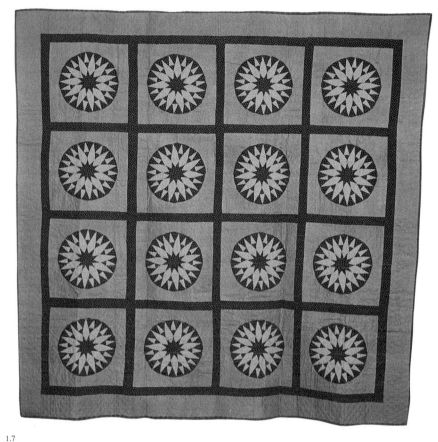

1.7

1.5

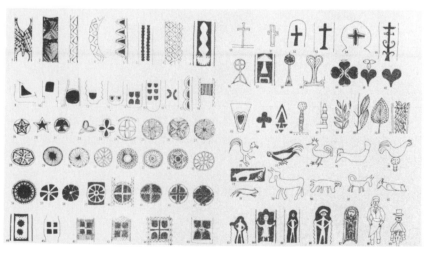

1.6

1.8

1.9

(figures 1.5, 1.6, and 1.7).[5] The most radical German Protestants leaned closest to the primitive love of abstraction. Traditional Lutherans, on the other hand, enjoyed realistic Christian images, and, with the moderate Reformed and many of the Anabaptist persuasion, embraced natural designs which symbolized rebirth—the adult commitment to "the good life." As a result, not only bars and squares and crowns, but flowers, fruitful trees, and hearts bearing blooms and seed pods (symbolizing the three stages from birth to rebirth—that is, purification,

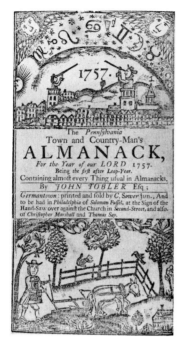

1.10

1.11. Woodcut from Martin Luther's "September Bible" (first Wittenberg edition of 1522). The woodcut is accompanied by the reference, "Earthquake and Signs in the Sun, Moon, and Stars" taken from Revelations 6:12-17: "And I beheld when he had opened the sixth seal, and, lo, there was a great earthquake; and the sun became black as sackcloth of hair, and the moon became as blood; and the stars of heaven fell unto the earth, even as a fig tree casteth her untimely figs, when she is shaken of a mighty wind." The woodcut and the text remind us of the power of the heavenly elements as Christian symbols of divine judgment. Illustrated in Kenneth A. Strand's *Reformation Bible Pictures* (Ann Arbor, Michigan: Ann Arbor Publishers, 1963).

1.11

enlightenment, and union) were keys to their religion and to their quilts (figures 1.8 and 1.9).[6]

Despite the risk of overgeneralization and specific instances which contradict these connections between religion and design, a little history of group tastes uncovers theological reasons for Lutheran, Reformed, and sectarian aesthetic preferences. Knowing that early radical Protestants objected to visual art—especially the public image—and furiously destroyed the art of the church provides the context for the

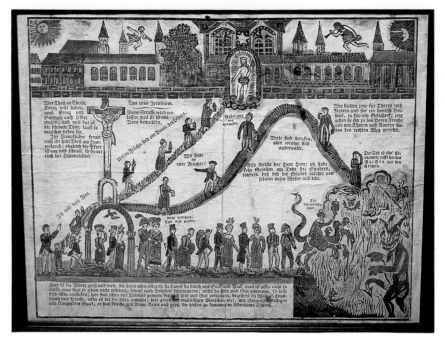

1.12

1.12. Broadside, Lutheran, editions printed 1827-47, Harrisburg; Gustav Sigismund Peters, printer. The emblem books which Pennsylvania Germans kept next to their bibles and the broadsides, or prints, which they had hanging on their walls, displayed the sun, moon, and stars set precariously above the New Jerusalem. In this broadside, heaven and hell are represented as the roads leading to either everlasting life or eternal damnation. Collection of Mr. and Mrs. Victor L. Johnson; photograph by Ken White.

1.13. Star, pieced and appliquéd quilt, possibly Lutheran, c. 1900, locale unknown. Maker unknown. 71" square. Cotton materials in dark blue, maroon, and gold with prints of red and white patches. Simple quilting. With the strong religious culture of the Germans in word and image, it is not surprising that Pennsylvania Germans worked images of the sun, moon, and stars into their quilts and other needlework. And as long as these images were tied to religious content, even the radical sects could ignore the Second Commandment against image-making. Collection of Robert L. Schaeffer, Jr., in Permanent Collection, Franklin and Marshall College; photograph by Ken White.

Pennsylvania sects' position (and, to a slightly lesser extent, the Reformed position of Zwingli and Calvin) against image-making. However, Luther, a churchly Protestant, saw nothing wrong with natural or representative art. He recognized that "ordinary people were caught more easily by analogies and illustrations than by difficult and subtle discussions."[7] He thought people would rather look at a well-drawn picture than read a well-written book. For him it was the art patron trying to buy salvation with purchases of art for the church, and not art itself, that was to be condemned. We can reasonably expect Lutheran quilters, therefore, to have preferred realistic images, especially if they could be tied to moral or churchly messages.[8] Symbols of the crown, the heart, the flower, the bird, and the lamb were unequivocally acceptable for Lutheran quilters who wanted to use them.

Heavenly bodies as artistic signs were also acceptable to Lutherans and can be traced back to Luther's own edition of the Bible, to the vernacular German fraktur and broadsides, to emblem books such as the very popular one compiled by Lutheran pastor Johann Arndt and published by Benjamin Franklin, and to almanacs like Tobler's published by Christopher Sower, Jr., in Germantown (figures 1.10, 1.11, and 1.12). Astronomical signs such as the rising sun (associated with the rooster welcoming the dawn of resurrection) were also found on the Pennsylvania-German quilt, as were the moon's phases, which had always been intrinsic to the South Germans of the Palatinate, Wurtemberg, and Switzerland (figure 1.13).[9] The sun, the moon, and the stars, described in the Bible as exerting more than natural upheavals

1.13

on earth (Revelation 6:12-17), indicated divine power, which some took
to occult extremes. There was for many Pennsylvania Germans a
"proper" juxtaposition of stars and planets at birth and on important
occasions which coincided with the seasons, agricultural operations,
and the four "medical" humors. Nature, man, and the calendar were
one. As Philadelphia Quaker Christopher Marshall noted in his journal
of 1780, Germans in his area forbade the popular medical treatment of

blood-letting on Ascension Day. And many quilters knew not to sew on Ascension Day.[10]

Zwingli, the Reformed leader preceding Calvin, also had a strong but learned position on the subject of art. Being an accomplished musician, he appreciated the sense of beautiful sound, but, being a reformer, he believed art was good only if it remained private. An audience, he thought, gave art a stigma by encouraging hypocrisy and display.[11] The making of a quilt, like unaccompanied psalm singing, could have been considered a form of private worship because the craft was able to be accomplished at home. Zwingli made "home" justify the senses and the visual and musical arts. The hidden meaning was kept at home, too, away from critical eyes. If they were domestic and private, gifts of art to God were rarely idolatrous to believers in the Reformed tradition.

At first, the radical sects of Amish and Mennonites, with their focus on mysticism, gave Germans and German products trouble in the American-Anglican community. German mysticism in America increased the general suspicion that Palatinate people, particularly the sects which did not require an educated ministry, were partial to the Catholic mystics and incidentally to the French. Even the churchly Pennsylvania-German Lutherans and Reformed joined their English neighbors in criticizing the lack of trained, recognized clergy among Pennsylvania-German sectarians. According to traditional Protestants, simple family leadership was not considered sufficiently religious to ward off Jesuit persuasion or to guide and protect God and family.[12]

The sects were outsiders in Europe and in America. Feeling like an outsider of course alters the rules, the reading, and the art a sect member will embrace. The Mennonite and Amish groups rejected regular organization, most sacraments and creeds, and introduced their own norms of authority. Rejecting union of church and state, they went back in theory to the days before Constantine when the church stood alone. A few sects saw themselves as having begun in the days of the Apostles. The Reformation sectaries focused on a primitive return to Jesus and Abraham with emphasis on the "inner word" rather than the "outer word" or human learning of Luther, Zwingli, and Calvin.[13] Sects believed each day's work was their sacrament. And it was these Mennonites, coming out of medieval sectarianism and the Reformed movement of Zwingli and Menno Simons (Anabaptists of the Swiss-South German group) who composed the largest number of sectarians in Colonial Pennsylvania.[14] (The term "Mennonite" was also used by the urban Dutch-North Germans and Russians who came to America in the 1870s.)

If any scholar has dealt in detail with these Swiss-German sects and the mysticism they planted in American soil it has been John Joseph Stoudt. Working in the 1930s with Roland Bainton of Yale and Henry Snyder Gehman of Princeton, Stoudt defiantly linked medieval

1.14

1.14. The inscription on this 1810 bookmark from southeastern Pennsylvania reads (in English translation): "O noble heart, ponder thy end," a text common to Mennonites. Schwenkfelders, and some Mennonites, used the image of the "Noble Heart," the symbolic source of all spiritual flowering, in their artistic endeavors. Collection of Philadelphia Free Library; photograph by Joan Broderick.

1.15. Detail, pieced and appliquéd signature quilt made for Mrs. Anora Richards, wife of Pastor John William Richards of St. Michael's Lutheran Church, Germantown. Lilies of the valley and the biblical inscription, "Consider the lilies of the field," are drawn in ink on the patch contributed by Mary M. Homiller. Collection of Germantown Historical Society; photograph by Ken White.

1.16. A detail from the same signature quilt. A scroll with flowers and leaves and the inscription, "He clothe the lilly of the field," are drawn in ink on the patch contributed by Elizabeth Root. The lily reflects the belief in a paradaisical new-birth in the heart of man. Churchly quilters were particularly aware of biblical texts.

1.15   1.16

iconography to all the Protestant Reformers. He declared that the cultural elite of Greeks, Hebrews, and Italians influenced ordinary American Anabaptists at the Ephreta Cloister, Moravian Brethren in Bethlehem, and Schwenkfelders in Montgomery County.[15] In his book *Consider the Lilies How They Grow*, Stoudt identified the Silesian Jacob Boehme as the man who turned the formal scriptural garden allegory into a peasant tradition. Boehme insisted that the sectarians of his time recognized at least two visual signs of "the good life"—the rose of Sharon and the lily of the valley. And he indicated that the sectarian mystic as well as the cultivated Protestant insider was aware of the rose as Jesus who ". . . shall come again on earth when life is perfect (when the lily blooms), in the fragrant springtime of the paradaisical new-birth in the heart of man" (figure 1.14).[16]

Except for the Amish sect, German-American Protestants coming out of Middle Europe shared a devotion to the allegory of the natural flower and particularly the lily. As late as 1844, for example, the ladies of St. Michael's Lutheran Church of Germantown pieced a friendship quilt for their pastor's wife with the biblical phrase from Matthew 6:28-30, "Consider the lilies," embroidered on one patch and "he clothe[d] the

1.17. Fraktur, attributed to David Huebner (Heebner) and very like Susanna Heebner's fraktur garden. Schwenkfelder, early nineteenth century, probably Montgomery County. The garden and its flowers, trees, fruits, and animals functioned since the days of illuminated manuscripts as symbols of the good life. Churchly craftspeople as well as the Schwenkfelder and Moravian sects made considerable use of these representational motifs. For a complete analysis of this fraktur's garden as a symbol for Mary, see Peter Erb's lecture printed for the Society for German-American Studies, Schwenkfelder Library. Collection of Schwenkfelder Library; photograph courtesy Philadelphia Museum of Art.

1.18. Fraktur of Mary and Jesus with a text by Martin Luther, Lutheran, c. 1830, southeastern Pennsylvania. Geographically, the closer Germans moved towards Catholic Maryland, the more they tended to use realistic images for their crafts, including quilting. Collection of Philadelphia Free Library; photograph by Joan Broderick.

1.18   1.17

1.19

1.19. Detail, Whig Rose (variation), appliquéd quilt, c. 1850, locale unknown. Maker unknown. 98" x 96". Solid-color cotton materials in white, orange, green, red, and yellow; prints in green, pink, and blue and yellow. Quilting in a star design is found in the white background; quilting in a feather pattern is worked in the border. The lily and the rose remained emblems of great moral and spiritual significance for Pennsylvania-German quilters and emblem writers. Collection of Mr. and Mrs. Victor L. Johnson; photograph by Ken White.

lilly [sic] of the field" embroidered on another (figures 1.15 and 1.16). This quilt text, like others of its kind, suggests the biblical awareness of churchly quilting craftswomen. They knew and accepted the medieval mystic's connotation of the lily as a beautiful flower which, like the dedicated believer, did not earn beauty but received it as a gift from God.

There are of course naturalistic symbols other than the lily found on many Pennsylvania-German quilts. The rose, tree, fruits, birds, and animals of the garden functioned as churchly symbols as well as signs for Brethren (Dunkards) and Schwenkfelders (figure 1.17). The closer the quilters moved toward Catholic Maryland the more they tended to use these realistic and natural signs (figure 1.18). Their patterns of settlement seemed thus to parallel and perhaps influence their quilt patterns. The farther south the quilters went the more they were exposed to the literal and traditional cross, crucifixion, rampant lamb, and Mary and Child iconography used by Catholics and some high-church Lutherans (figure 1.19).

Many in the exlusive minorities of Amish and Mennonites eventually moved to the more distant and vaguely settled West. They preferred the quilt pattern language of geometry which was equally distant and

1.20. Joseph's Coat, pieced quilt, Mennonite, c. 1900, Lititz. Made by a Mrs. Franck for her son Henry. Approximately 72" x 74". Cotton materials in blue, green, white, yellow, red, and purple. The bars are enclosed by a striped border. The vagaries of abstraction seem to parallel the vague and distant West, where many of the exclusive minorities of Mennonites and Amish moved. Their quilt patterns reflect a protective geometric privacy. Photograph courtesy of M. Finkel and Daughter, Inc.

1.20

vague. It is not coincidental that a people considered to be outsiders should avoid the city, avoid acculturation, and avoid traditional Christian designs. This context helps to explain the preference for the protection of abstraction and geometry which make messages harden to decipher and therefore easier to keep private. With their instinctive and unconscious need for liturgical color and their conscious literary pattern titles which replaced any representational designs, the Amish and the Mennonites could still keep their biblically oriented people in touch with The Word. The Amish named the zigzag line "Path of Thorns." They called one series of triangular arrangements "Crown of Thorns" and a set of rising, covering blocks Bunyan's "Delectable Mountains" (figure 3.62). Mennonites labeled one type of vertical bar pattern "Joseph's Coat" (figure 1.20) and one type of diagonal bar with diamonds "Jacob's Ladder" (figure 3.82).

Scholars who look for sociological, cultural, religious, or sexist meaning in quilt designs have been criticized today by some quilters of being too much with the book and too little with the object. And art critics, too, have resented the search in quilts for anything more than sensual pleasure and what is called "the beautiful." The study of material culture and aesthetics certainly provides important views on the products of every century. And one would never deny the position of the actual craftsperson at work who explained his or her pleasure in

1.21

1.22

1.21. Redware dish (three tulips in pot), sgraffito decoration, Schwenkfelder and Reformed, 1785-86, Upper Hanover Township, Montgomery County. Attributed to George Huebner (Heebner). Like quilters, Pennsylvania-German potters inscribed their works with matters close to their hearts—religion. The German inscription on this dish reads (in translation): "No plaster can heal me, so you will want to hurry with me from this world into the canopy of heaven." Collection of Philadelphia Museum of Art.

1.22. Wardrobe, probably Reformed, dated 1779, Manheim and Warwick townships, Lancaster County. Attributed to Peter Holl and Christian Huber. Furniture such as this Pennsylvania-German wardrobe contains inlaid motifs, similar to quilting motifs, which tie the culture and religion of the craftsperson to his product. Included in this piece are such churchly motifs as crown and cross, six-pointed stars, birds, swastikas, and pots of flowers. Collection of the Philadelphia Museum of Art.

1.23. Dower chest over drawers, probably Lutheran, dated 1818, Centre County. Made for George Corman. The painted eagle resembles the bird on the Graby-Risser quilt shown in figure 2.14. It also resembles the eagle on the reverse of the 1798 ten-dollar gold piece. Surrounded, however, by swastika and compass motifs and holding in its talons tulips instead of arrows and laurel leaves, it can be best identified as a Pennsylvania-German design rather than a patriotic symbol. This eagle is a crucial link between the medieval past and the nineteenth century, between Germany and America, between the Old Church, the Reformation, and the Reformed.

1.24. Sampler, probably Lutheran, dated 1822, Lancaster County. Made by Catherine Esbenshade. The memorial inscription invokes the spirit of emroiderers and quilters alike: ". . . awake, asleep, at home abroad, I am surrounded still with God . . . When I am dead and laid in my grave and all my bones are rotten, remember me when this you see least I should be forgotten." Like the quilter, this needleworker wanted to communicate with designs and words the importance of "preparation for the life that now is . . . [and] for the life to come." Among the stitched motifs are swastika, tulip, eagle, and variable star. Collection of Philip Bradley Antiques; photograph by George Fistrovich, Winterthur Museum.

1.23

1.24

creating objects.

For some quilters, too, their work was no more than a set of patches done in free time for fun or fashion. And this may have been all the more possible in the twentieth century. But it was not the case for most German craftspeople in history to work without putting a bit of their better philosophy into their objects. Like eighteenth-century potter George Huebner, who very crudely scribed on one of his dishes, "No plaster can heal me, so you will want to hurry with me from this world into the canopy of heaven," the German craftsperson believed that even simple art and earthly textures could convey deep commitment to eternal life (figure 1.21).

The story of the Pennsylvania-German quilt continues in the next chapter with German life in the counties and churches of southeastern and central Pennsylvania, exhibiting more of the symbolically embellished materials that surrounded them at home. Quilts, as furniture and samplers do, make visible to us certain churchly and sectarian theological assumptions about art (figures 1.22, 1.23, and 1.24). Despite their beauty, quilts transmit data and show the quilter's mind as well as her heart, her ability to think or "have sense" as well as to feel or "to sense." This book emphasizes the fact that the quilter wanted to communicate as well as to please and wanted to communicate what H. A. Muhlenberg declared was the central German spirit in America. He described it in 1836 "as preeminently a religious one, which looked not only at the intellect but the soul, and had in mind not only the preparation for the life that now is but for the life to come."[17]

2. Quilt Patterns as Part of American History

LIKE ALL PENNSYLVANIA ART, which Frank Sommer, librarian of the Henry Francis du Pont Winterthur Museum, calls distinctive adaptations and transformations of medieval thought, Pennsylvania quilt patterns are distinctive and adaptive. Developing as a quilting stitch or as a pieced or applied patch, designs emerged in geographical and religious pockets, particularly in the south and central Pennsylvania counties where specific religious groups settled. The earliest community of Germantown and, soon after, Chester and Lancaster counties, functioned as uneasy but interdependent networks of English and German settlers with craftspeople sharing work, ministers sharing pulpits, and quilters sharing needlework designs (figure 3.66). Such unions forced accommodation of all sorts, economic, religious, social, and artistic. But adaptation was the aesthetic and philosophical underpinning of what today we like to call the American style or the American taste.

But how, then, can we look back not only at the medieval antecedents but at this very American, democratic crossing of cultures and isolate a quilt pattern and say with any assurance that it is Pennsylvania-German? Some quilt researchers identify German quilts by locating their donor or current owner and by data obtained through oral family histories and present-day quilters. Each of these avenues in our material culture advances the accuracy of understanding the art of the quilt in America. Social historians are aware that the quilt is more than a work of art without a text. This author has chosen to look at the Pennsylvania quilt as an aspect of German and Reformed theology, despite the American resistance to thinking about art and church, which is almost as ingrained as thinking about state and church. In fact, implicit in Hebraic and Protestant theology generally is the resistance of using art and religion toward the same end. The development of democracies and museums originally stemmed from the need to separate "the non-negotiable hierarchies of the spiritual world" from the civil world and the art world.[1]

The identification of a historical craftsperson's religious preferences, for example, can help students of American decorative arts to isolate

25

what is English or German about pieces of Pennsylvania furniture. Once familiar with national iconographic preferences, it becomes possible, say, to examine a tall case clock made in the English settlement of Bucks County, which contains inlay designed in the German cabinetmaking taste, and know that though the piece was made in the English county of Bucks it incorporated distinct Germanic references (figure 2.1). This understanding keeps the researcher from deciding too quickly on geographical grounds alone that the furniture form was made by an English cabinetmaker.

Social historians can see patrons as well as craftspeople in mixed settlements being satisfied with a desk created with English high-style interior carving and German star, crown, and tulip (lily) inlay (figure 2.2). And, once alert to the Germanic motifs, samplers (figure 1.24) and many pieced quilts (figures 2.3, 3.66, 3.67, and 3.68) suddenly join the clock case and desk in sharing an art history of mixed origin but broadly understood to be Pennsylvania-German and quite possibly churchly or sectarian. Though the pieced quilt was technically an English needlework tradition derived from Indian and Persian textiles, with designs rooted in the medieval spirit, Germans settling in the English colony of Pennsylvania adopted the craft as their own.[2] But, in designing quilts, they filtered out and reproduced only what was meaningful to their German religion and culture. Even when they borrowed the designs of their neighbors, they did so in "a group way," that is, they settled down in certain counties of Pennsylvania by church affiliation and worked motifs to which their group implicitly gave approval. It is this group approval and the motifs that seemed to accommodate their overriding spiritual tenets which the present chapter mainly attempts to identify.

2.2

2.1

26

2.1. Tall-case clock, dated 1787, New Britain, Bucks County. Made by Banjamin Morris for "A. I." Very German and churchly lilies, stars, and a crown, with other petalled flowers and the date, are inlaid either across the hood, the waist, or the plinth of the clock case. Though the mechanism of the clock was inscribed by a craftsman of English descent, the symbols in the wood inlay indicate that the case was in all probability made by a Pennsylvania German. Private collection; photograph courtesy of Israel Sack, Inc.

2.2. Detail, slant-top desk, probably Lutheran or Reformed, dated 1771, Chester or Lancaster County. Maker unknown. Furniture from areas settled by adaptive English and German craftsmen often reflects the blending of these two cultures. This desk with English high-style interior carving is also inlaid with the star, crown, tulip (lily), and dove, symbols typically embraced by religious Germans. Photograph courtesy of Israel Sack, Inc.

German settlements in Pennsylvania began in 1683 when William Penn sold 6000 acres north and west of Philadelphia to Mennonites agented by the Lutheran pietist Francis Daniel Pastorius.[3] Of the first thirteen settlers of Germantown, eleven were of the Mennonite sect, and two were of the Reformed Church. Dunkards (German Baptists or Brethren), Lutherans, and Moravians followed them to Germantown.[4] The Lutherans and Reformed were city as well as country people in the Palatinate and in Pennsylvania. Many of them were receptive to English taste, English language, English prayers, and to the accepted English structure of life in the new colony. They understood well the union of church and state, seeing the English king, George II, was a German and his court chaplain a Lutheran pastor.[5]

The Moravians were a strange bridge between the more traditional Lutheran insiders and the less defined communal Anabaptist outsiders. Moravians influenced John Wesley and his newly created English Methodism. Though a sect, Moravians approved of higher education, training of women, and the inclusion of non-Moravians in their seminary in Bethlehem. English ladies who sent their daughters to the Moravian school insisted the tutoresses be well-bred and educated. And though Moravians were country people, the tutoresses did not pass on the sect's "rusticity" to students.[6] In 1787 Moravians were the only sect included with the churchly Lutherans, Reformed, Episcopalians, Presbyterians, and Catholics on the board of trustees of Franklin College, a college intended to educate Germans to English culture and taste. Moravian views on education, then, create the same confusing puzzle as do Moravian quilts and samplers. Were they plain or were they fancy?

The Anabaptist-derived sects, however, quickly set themselves as far apart as they could from the English and other Germans, whether in regard to language, infant baptism, loyalty to the state, or symbolic design.[7] They quickly settled more purely German communities. Their secludedness has been a boon to quilt scholars and Americans who embrace Mennonite and Amish quilts with a kind of reverence. Is it their sectarianness, their exclusiveness, their defiance and resistance that we admire most? Is their stark symbolism, saying very little which is concrete and thereby mystifying us, the real reason for our fascination?

These smaller picturesque sects from Germantown soon moved out to Lancaster County (figure 2.4). In two of the county towns, the Mennonites quickly outnumbered all the other denominations. The Dunkards moved to Montgomery, Berks, and Lancaster counties and later to Dauphin and Lebanon counties. In 1724 Conrad Beissel, a Dunkard, enlisted the help of a German Reformed minister and a German Lutheran to organize the Seventh Day Baptists at Ephrata in Lancaster County.[8] Forty families of Schwenkfelders (Lutheran-

27

2.3

2.3. Pieced and appliquéd signature quilt, Mennonite, c. 1848, Johnsville, Bucks County. Made by members of the Althouse family and friends for Mrs. Jacob Krewson. 102" square. Cotton materials in red, green, blue, yellow, and brown. Among the patterns included are Fleur-de-lis, Reel and Orange Peel, four types of Variable Star, Lone Star, Nine-Patch, and Rolling Stone. Such presentation quilts were usually stitched for an important member of the community, often the minister or his wife associated with the church with which the quilters were affiliated. Collection of The Mercer Museum of The Bucks County Historical Society.

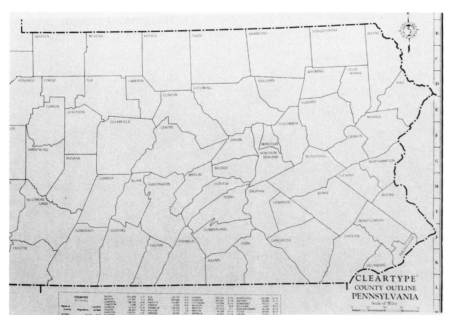

2.4

2.4. County map of German settlements, showing the integrated counties of Philadelphia, Montgomery, and Chester and also the more Solidly German counties of Lancaster, Berks, York, and Dauphin. Geography, like theology, is a clue to some quilting design elements. For cosmopolitan German Reformed and Lutherans who stayed in the cities, motifs ranged from maturalistic to celestial. For exclusive minorities who moved to surrounding counties, the preferred motifs ranged from celestial to abstract. Photograph courtesy American Map Corporation, Clear Type County Outline Pennsylvania.

derived) reached Philadelphia in 1734 and promptly left for Montgomery, Bucks, Berks, and Lehigh counties. The Amish emigrated in 1727. They went to Berks and Lancaster counties in the 1740s and to Somerset and Mifflin counties in the 1760s.[9]

What happened to the more numerous German Reformed and Lutheran groups? Some of the Reformed stayed in Germantown and built the first German Reformed church in 1719. Some of them moved to Montgomery and Berks counties in 1725 and later with the Lutherans to York and the counties of central Pennsylvania—Dauphin, Clinton, Union, Northumberland, Lycoming, Snyder, and Centre. Though the Reformed groups kept close ties with the Dutch Church in Holland and maintained a Presbyterian form of organization, the German Reformed people were most like the Lutherans. Historian William Sweet reminds us that they were alike "in doctrine and worship and lived and worked harmoniously together."[10]

In her books on Pennsylvania quilts Jeannette Lasansky notes that church Germans were alike in their taste for red and green prints, which some still properly call calico, and in their preference that their good needlewomen work the more elaborate quilting designs. Naturalistic garden motifs of flowers and fruits were among the designs churchly quilters chose. They liked using red- and green-colored fabrics for applied patches and sometimes pink and green cloth for pieced ones. Germans from Columbia, Perry, and Cumberland counties also appliquéd the red-green rose and bud wreath or branch.

Our modern fascination with the work of the Mennonites and the Amish does not erase the fact that Lutherans were the most numerous of all the German religious groups in America. Henry Melchior Muhlenberg, their most famous pastor, presided over Germantown, Montgomery, and the later Lancaster, Berks, and York churches. He organized the first Lutheran synod in America at St. Michael's Church in Philadelphia in 1748, teaching mild pietism to an essentially cosmopolitan community. Though American Lutherans included Danes, Swedes, and Norwegians, historically it was the German Lutherans who poured into America from 1720 onward and who swelled the conservative Lutheran population during our "quilt era" between 1830 and 1870.[11] They had large congregations in Germantown and in Montgomery County. Other Lutherans settled in Union, Berks, Lancaster, and Lehigh counties. Their settlement in Berks County amounted to ninety percent of the population and enabled Lancaster, Lehigh, and York counties to become sixty percent German by 1860.[12]

By the mid-nineteenth century, when patched or pieced quilting was an established Pennsylvania-German tradition and when the sewing machine reached the marketplece, tempting the quilter's devotion to pure handicrafts, the era of American nationalism ended and the era of

American sectionalism began. Americans were now more interested in their county than in their country. Correspondingly, each denomination began to focus on its own specific concerns. As William Sweet writes, "Loyalty to a denomination comes now to be the great emphasis, just as loyalty to the South or the North became the catchword in politics."[13] And with this general turning inward went an emphasis on conservatism even among the cosmopolitan Lutherans. Lutheran immigrants, after all, had left Europe in the nineteenth century not because of persecution, but to escape the liberal and rationalistic ways of their state church They added to America's orthodoxy and enhanced reliance on medieval symbolism and pietism which increased the high time of the quilt.

Lutheran pietists then joined Anabaptist sects in leaning on what Luther himself had once complained was the "carnal" or subjective sense in a person, one's excessive reliance on the heart instead of the head.[14] For nineteenth-century Mennonite, Amish, Schwenkfelder, and Dunkard, "the cloven hoof"—the double meaning in the Bible—remained the way to interpret motifs whether written, drawn, painted, or sewn. And as a recognized Lutheran pietist wrote in 1854, Lutherans must accept "all the symbolical books as the pure and uncorrupted explanation and statement of the Divine Word. . . . "[15] Evangelical "awakenings," occurring in nineteenth-century America, drove quilters like everyone else toward purifying their communities, centering on activities like quilting which, though domestic, made public statements aimed at creating a better world.

Fund-raising and presentation quilts, which are essentially signature quilts, reflected this new social, quasi-religious conservatism. Event-oriented quilts flourished "among nineteenth-century evangelical Protestant women who joined forces to spread the Gospel, help the needy, and protect their homes from the threats posed by an increasingly complex society."[16] And, whether they quilted for the church, for abolitionist or temperance reform, these women made strong statements about society, about themselves, and about the importance of quilts, the latter of which amazingly has never diminished (figures 2.5, 2.6, 2.7, 2.8). Form did not come without content for the evangelical woman. She used form to make a social statement and to embody her own private spirit. And like a true artist, who always expresses affection and love, she expressed what the Pennsylvania-German woman loved the most—symbols of birth and rebirth.[17]

Signature quilts, sometimes called album (many makers) or friendship quilts (usually one maker), often came from the church tradition rather than from the sects (figure 2.9). Sect women, having fewer worldly interests, tended to avoid national issues and explicit content. They rarely had professional clergy for whom many of the signature quilts

2.5. Detail, Nine-Patch with Lilies, pieced signature quilt, Lutheran, dated 1842, York County. Maker unknown. Made for the wife of the Rev. Dr. Augustus H. Lochman, former pastor of Christ Lutheran Church. 98" x 92". Cotton materials in red and white patches, each of which includes an inscription and the name of a friend. Event-oriented quilts flourished "among nineteenth-century evangelical Protestant women who joined forces to spread the Gospel, help the needy, and protect their homes from the threats posed by an increasingly complex society." Photograph courtesy of the Historical Society of York County, Pennsylvania.

2.5

were made.[18] The churchly Lutherans took the strong statement of red (the color of communion) and the spiritually meaningful contrast of red and white patches and embroidery thread to make the nine-patch, chimney sweep, triangular and circular motifs for their pastors (figures 2.5 and 2.6). The Salem Church ladies of Snyder County embroidered religious inscriptions along with fund-raisers' names. One inscription reveals what many thought was the mysticism of the quilt itself: "I speak though I am silent."[19] Quilters for Ray's Lutheran Church in Union County and ladies of a York Lutheran church used names embroidered in red floss to create compass-type designs. Presbyterians and Methodists, too, used red floss and patches for church quilts. They all must have appreciated the colorfast quality of the new red thread touted in the late nineteenth century by *The Ladies' Home Journal*.[20]

Though the Mennonites worked only a few signature quilts, the Kriebel

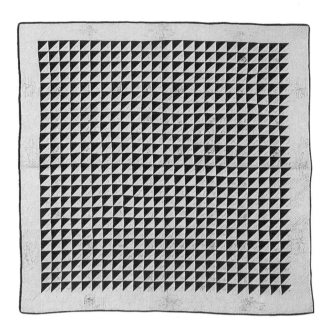

2.7

2.6. Pieced signature quilt, Lutheran, c. 1883, York County. Made by friends as a Christmas gift to the Rev. Aaron Spangler. Cotton materials in red and white. A signature quilt, often used for fund-raising, was sometimes called a beddelman or beggarman quilt, since money was requested for each name inscribed. The names here were inscribed on the white triangles in brown ink. Churchly Lutherans often used red, the color of communion, with contrasting white patches and embroidery thread to create the Nine-Patch, Chimney Sweep, triangular and circular motifs for such signature quilts. Photograph courtesy of the Historical Society of York County, Pennsylvania.

2.7. Detail, Bird and Tree (with Variable Star); pieced, appliquéd, and embroidered wedding quilt. Moravian, c. 1815, Northeast Bethlehem, Northampton County. Made by Christiana Schafer (or Scheifer) Kichline. 82" x 87". Cotton materials in prints of red and white, crewel wools, and red and green wool fringe. Hand-quilting follows the pieced design; chain stitch embroidery. The wools for this quilt were dyed and carded by the maker, who also worked two pillow shams to match her quilt. The set was owned by the Unangst family. Generally the image of birds was too naturalistic for sectarians to use on quilts. Collection of

2.8

2.8. Pieced signature quilt, Mennonite, dated 1897, Bally, Berks County. Made by Mary Gehman Kriebel. Dimensions unknown. Cotton materials in rust with red, maroon, yellow, light blue, and black. Black and brown border; nine-patch squares set in corners The sashing and square separations are typical of Mennonite work. Some of the patterns included are Swastika, Basket, Bow-Tie, Compass, Bear's Paw, Variable Star, Nine-Patch, Log Cabin, Capital T (for temperance), and Rolling Stone. This signature quilt probably developed as a friendship quilt, since few sect women had worldly interests and avoided national issues and explicit content. Collection of Lydia G. Kriebel on loan to the Mennonite Heritage Center; photograph courtesy of John W. Munro, Harleysville, Pennsylvania.

album, made ln 1893, was designed by a Mennonite woman who married a Schwenkfelder man (figure 2.8). Typical of Mennonite quilters, she chose mostly straight-lined abstract designs, but, like her life, the quilt contained many variations. Among them were the variable star, the swastika, the compass, the nine- and sixteen-patch squares, the basket, chimney sweep, log cabin, and bow-tie or hourglass motifs. She was unlike the Amish Mennonite quilters for whom friendship with the world was not a priority of art or religious conviction.

Mennonites and Schwenkfelders from Bucks and Montgomery counties leaned favorably toward the domestic basket design. Though Pennsylvania Amish quilters consciously refrained from employing realistic images, the few who chose the basket design tended to select a geometric or straight-line handle (figure 2.10) as opposed to Mennonites who were freer to choose the more sensual, more sentimental curved handle (figures 2.11 and 3.1). This choice necessitated appliqué, which technically was more difficult and more fancy than plain In contrast to the curve, a straight line is philosophically more abstract and more defensive. In Émile Mâle's history of religious art, for example, we discover that "linear structure [and] the angular attitudes [generally] convey no idea of life."[21] A more equalizing attitude toward straightness and curves was taken by a contemporary New England Calvinist poet who wrote, "Straight is the path of duty/Curved is the path of beauty."[22]

The basket motif is a good example of the difference between the way those in our own materialistic and secular age may look at a basket patch and the way many looked at it in the age preceding us. Even with Freud's reminder that every choice we make implies a condition we want to communicate, we look at a basket today and usually see just a basket. But in the nineteenth-century age of evangelicalism and German Romanticism, pietists generally believed that designs meant more than the eye made of them. The basket, like the cornucopia, spelled out domestic and spiritual abundance and sometimes recalled the "ample basket full of hay at Jesus' nativity scene" which was introduced in the first Protestant era.[23] The Bible reminded pietists that though a basket could look empty and meaningless, as quilting basket motifs often did (figures 3.2 and 3.3), it might "feed the multitudes."

And nineteenth-century women from the Anabaptist to the Unitarian saw themselves as the benevolent feeders of the family and saw family religion as the divinely-approved method of reproducing Christian character.[24] Religious leaders, both professional and lay, saw in women some of these unusual powers associated with a deceptively empty yet ample basket. And in the history of art the basket has retained this optimistic, container-like, womanly reference to charity. The nineteenth-century quilter was not a barren Eve.

2.9

2.9. Pieced signature quilt, Lutheran or Reformed, c. 1850, Boyerstown, Berks County. Maker unknown. 85" x 88". Cotton materials in navy, red, and green; backing is a blue copperplate print. Some of the persons whose names are inscribed on the patches lived in different cities or towns. It is possible that the patches were made in different places and sent to a central quilter for assembly. More likely, considering the men's names and the use of identical materials, the squares were all made in one place by one person who inscribed the names out of friendship or in recognition of a financial contribution to a charity. Courtesy of Patricia Breidenbach Fedor on permanent loan to Boyertown Area Historical Society; photograph by Ken White.

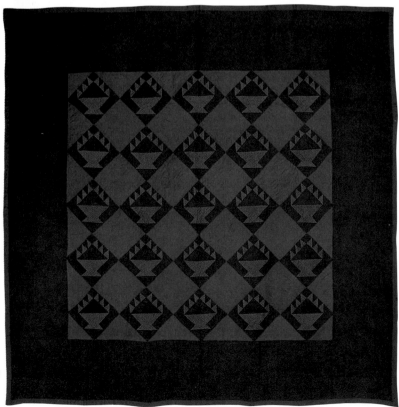

2.10

2.10. Baskets, pieced quilt, Amish, c. 1938, Lancaster County. Maker unknown. 78" x 80". Wool crepe materials in pink, two types of green, blue, and red. The green border is quilted in a flower pattern; a compass design is quilted in the solid-blue squares. Each basket is quilted in a shell pattern. The straight-line basket handle on this quilt is more abstract than natural and technically less difficult to work than the curved. But theologically and technically, the Amish opted for being plain rather than fancy. Collection of Dr. and Mrs. Donald M. Herr; photograph by Ken White.

2.11. Baskets, pieced and appliquéd quilt, Mennonite, c. 1880, locale unknown. Maker unknown. 72" square. Cotton materials in green, red, and yellow. In each basket the curved handle is applied to the pieced basket. The quilt exhibits the use of typical Mennonite sashing and square separations. Mennonites and Schwenkfelders from Bucks and Montgomery counties leaned favorably toward the basket design. They frequently chose the sensual curved handle as opposed to the Amish straight-line one. Photograph courtesy of M. Finkel and Daughter, Inc.

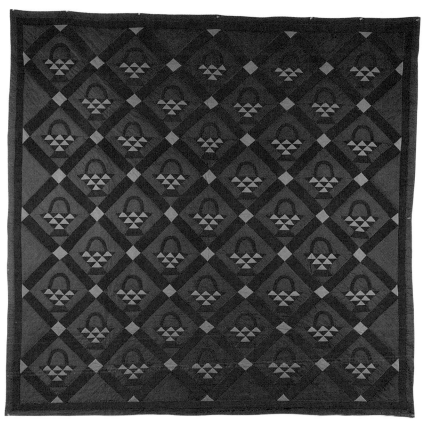

2.11

The leafy tree was another network of sacred references. Western culture has kept it as a symbol of life. Like the basket, the tree can be as abstract as the diamond or the square. And, like the basket, the tree has spiritually fruitful implications. In fact, like most of the flowers in a nineteenth-century garden, the tree form was often a symbol of the gift of grace rather than a realistic drawing of a functioning, producing tree.[25] Whether it was the Old Testament Tree of Knowledge with its two kinds of fruit (figure 3.4), or the New Testament Tree of Life (figure 2.12), scriptural trees were common to contemporary prints, bibles, and appliquéd quilts.

Bird and tree motifs are found on Berks and Northampton County Moravian quilts (figures 2.7 and 2.13). Ephrata Baptists and pietistic Lutherans used the symbol mystically on their fraktur. The mystic justified symbolic content by assuming secrecy protected the truth from vulgar interpretation. Clarity came only to the spiritually alert. Bird motifs share with cherubs and angels an ancient tradition of spiritual rather than material references. According to Mosaic law two white doves in a basket are offerings at birth, and for nineteenth-century German Anabaptists they were baptismal symbols drinking from the lily of spiritual life (figures 1.22 and 2.2).

But generally birds were too naturalistic for sectarians to use on quilts. The sects were rarely literal about art or the Bible, unlike the Lutherans and Reformed who employed realistic birds in their crafts. Churchly designers translated the dove type almost mechanically into the Holy Spirit of the Trinity or even the Annunciation to Mary. The eagle, an Old Testament type from Isaiah foreshadowing John and the Gospel in the New Testament, was synonymous with bringing believers closer to God.[2b] As Miss Espenshade, a German needleworker, embroidered on her Lancaster sampler below the motif of an eagle, "Within thy circling power i stand. On every side i find thy hand. Awake asleep at home abroad, I am surrounded still with god" (figure 1.24).

Quilters of the Reformed Church felt compatibility with the real power of the eagle (not a pacifist symbol), using it as a motif for one of their most exciting quilt forms (figure 2.14). There seems to be a clear connection between color and county in these eagle quilts. According to Patricia Herr, the strong orange and yellow background colors were employed by quilters in northern and central Pennsylvania counties (heavily populated by churchly groups). One can see, therefore, that motif, color, and county reflect the more literal Lutheran and Reformed taste. Reformed Church craftspeople, like the churchly English in America, worked the national as well as the Christian eagle into their needleworks, paintings, and furniture (figure 1.23).

Hearts were an element often found on baptismal fraktur drawn for the Lutherans and Reformed in Berks, Lancaster, and Northampton counties.[27] The sects, which did not believe in infant baptism and thus had no baptismal certificates, were still theologically partial to the heart as an image of religious fervor. It was their sense that it had power over thought. Many Mennonites inscribed on bookmarks or linens, "O noble heart, ponder thy end." Schwenkfelder bookmarks often displayed a flower rising out of a heart, signifying rebirth. One churchly quilter stitched the heart as if it came from inside the flower (figure 1.3). But the heart remained an elusive motif, being subtly stitched rather than brightly patched. We find scattered Lutheran examples (figure 2.15) and a few pieced Mennonite heart motifs (figures 2.16 and 3.9). Masonic quilts also used heart designs, but the obvious secrecy of the order's symbolic message system alarmed nineteenth-century conservative Christians in the same way that the papal "bleeding heart" and cross found on early watercolors and furniture in Catholic Europe alarmed the radical reformers.

And yet the most Catholic symbol of all—the Virgin Mary—surfaced in the symbol of the rose without thorns as well as in the violet, the lily, the lily of the valley (figure 1.15), the iris, the enclosed garden (figure 1.17), and "all that is most delicious in nature."[28] Mary was referred to as springtime, a garland of flowers that was a garland of virtue. Of course not all German Protestant women knew that they were reviving

2.12

2.12. Tree of Life, dated 1846, New York. Printed by J. Baillie. Printed under tree: "The Tree of Life which bare twelve manner of fruits, and yielded her fruit every month, and the Leaves of the Tree were for the healing of the Nations. Rev. XXII ver. 2." The tree was a natural religious symbol found on both churchly English and German prints. This print spells out the Christian connotations of the Tree of Life which are less easy to read when the tree pattern appears on quilts. Private collection; photograph by Ken White.

2.13. Detail Bird and Tree (with Reel and Orange Peel), pieced and embroidered quilt, Moravian, patch dated 1830, Northampton County. Made by or for "E. S." (embroidered on quilt). Dimensions unknown. Wool material, red twill weaves, and cotton material in white. Silk and wool embroidery threads. Knotted wool fringe. Birds and trees are found on Berks and Lehigh County Moravian quilts, on quilts worked by those in the churchly tradition, and among pietists of both sect and church who viewed these motifs mystically rather than literally. Collection of Dr. and Mrs. Donald M. Herr; photograph by Ken White.

2.13

Mary when they chose to stitch a lily or a rose. But in the nineteenth century they no longer had a taste for the unadorned seventeenth-century approach to women as the fallen daughters of Eve. They put on a reworked but pietistic halo of flowers and enjoyed the new respect being given to women. Woman's role, originally made more important by Mennonites in the sixteenth century, was enhanced in the nineteenth by German evangelical and aesthetic movements.[29]

The lily was of course the leading symbol of the young Virgin. Lilies, the source of the tulip design, were embraced by all Germans excluding the Amish, and put on just about everything (figures 2.17, 2.19, and 2.20). The lily, like the bird, symbolized beauty as a natural miracle rather than as an object created by work or as something which produced useful things in the earthly garden. Lily designs were woven into coverlets and worked on samplers, fraktur, furniture, and quilts, particularly among the Reformed and the Mennonites. The rose, the other essentially Marian flower, was found on the quilts of Schwenkfelders in Montgomery County and the Lutherans and Reformed of central Pennsylvania (figure 2.18).

If the pious woman was represented mystically by the lily and the rose,

2.14

2.14. Eagle, appliquéd quilt, Reformed, dated Nov. 7, 1928, Lancaster County. Made by Sarah Graby Risser for Floyd G. Risser. 79½" x 80". Cotton materials in yellow, red, gold, and green; zigzag red border. The back is pieced in red and yellow panels. Simple quilting outlines elements of the design, feather quilting fills the border. Brilliant orange and yellow backgrounds are common to quilts of northern Lancaster, Berks, and Lebanon counties. Sarah Risser's mother was a Mennonite; her father, a Reformed deacon as was her paternal grandfather. Collection of Dr. and Mrs. Donald M. Herr; photograph by Ken White.

she was also represented by the heavenly bodies—the single star of divine guidance called the Stella Maris (Star of the Sea), the twelve stars of Mary's crown, and the sun and the moon. The star as a type or symbol was, like all the heavenly bodies, historically part of the Anabaptist enthusiasm for shadow and light (figure 2.21).[30] On churchly quilts the star was often made to sparkle by its diamond template shapes (figure 2.22) and seemed literally to burst out and down to earth as if following the stars in Luther's "September" Bible (figure 1.11).[31] The star was the most popular quilt image in churchly central Pennsylvania. A few sectarians also worked these sparkling designs (figures 2.23 and 2.24), but, like Quakers, it was Germans living primarily in cities or mixed communities in mid-century who attempted the design.

The sunburst or compass often resembled the diamond-constructed star (figures 3.44 and 3.47). Mennonites liked to utilize the less complex red calico on white to create the illusion of a star within a sun (figure 2.25). A variation of the sun or compass design was the Robbing Peter to Pay Paul motif (figure 2.26). It resembled the quilting stitch Avril Colby calls the wineglass pattern. Worked by Lutherans in Lehigh County and in central Pennsylvania and by Mennonites in Montgomery County,

2.15. Heart, Bird, Leaf, and Fruit, appliquéd quilt, Lutheran, c. 1840, locale unknown. Made by members of the Easterday family. 79" square. White cotton and cotton prints of red, green, and yellow; the birds' feet and fruit stems are embroidered in blue. Feather quilting and leaf patterns are worked in the overall design. Curves rather than lines caused difficulty for quilters attempting the heart appliqué, which could be considered a fancy technique. When an Amish quilter wanted to include a heart, she stitched it as a quilting design, hidden from view. Collection of Joan Easterday, Conklin, Barton, Harbison, Reese; photograph by Ken White.

2.16. Detail, pieced signature quilt, Mennonite, c. 1862, locale unknown. Makers unknown. Made for William Gross. Dimensions unknown. Cotton materials in white, blue, rust, and black. The repeat pattern is known as Wild Goose Chase. Note that hearts are inscribed in the center three squares with blue backgrounds. The inscriptions, from top to bottom, read: "Sarah Godshalk," "The Property of William Gross," and "Anna Godshalk." Collection of Jean Stutzman on loan to the Mennonite Heritage Center.

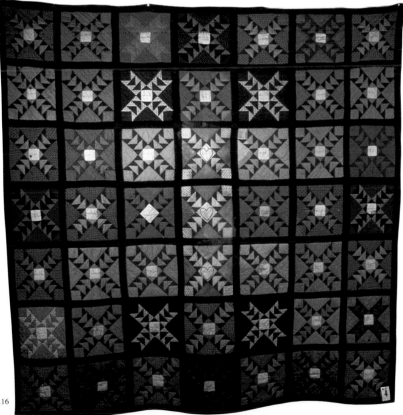

2.16

Robbing Peter to Pay Paul was one of the more difficult designs because of its curved lines, but was also one of the more popular motifs (figure 2.26).

Another variation of the circle enjoyed by Mennonites and Moravians was the reel design around which they usually flourished a leaf or orangle peel shape (figure 2.29). The reel was often chosen as a quilt design to commemorate the most formal occasions. Some Moravians and Mennonites used the reel for their crewel-worked bridal quilts (figures 2.13 and 3.52), and the Lutherans at St. Michael's Church in Germantown used the reel to complement their monumental biblical signature quilt. A unique variation of the reel, sometimes called Caesar's Crown and sometimes merely The Crown, was chosen by Lutheran women for events warranting a crown (figure 3.50). An 1849 quilt with exquisite trapunto or stuffed quilting patterns of flowers, eagle, and crown emphasizes the taste of Lutheran Church women for technically elaborate and realistically designed stitching and patch motifs (figure 3.51).

The last quarter of the nineteenth century found some quilters objecting to the elaborate bursting stars and suns on textile art. Twelve years after the Centennial of 1876, *Good Housekeeping* published a statement indicating the desire of women to go back to simple thoughts, designs, and materials—-as if "simple" meant "true" and perhaps "English Colonial." "When I say quilts," the author wrote, "I do not mean the gay red, green, and yellow abominations known as the 'Rising Star' and 'Setting Sun' that we see year after year exhibited at the country fair, but the modest 'Hexagon,' 'Ninepatch.' '[Variable or small] Star,' and 'Irish Chain' that we were taught to make when we were wee lassies."

2.17. Detail, appliquéd presentation quilt, Reformed, dated 1847, Harrisburg, Dauphin County. Made by thirty-six Salem Church members. Among the names inscribed are Bombaugh, Bucher, Gross, Hover, Kelner, Shrom, and Wolf. Made for Dr. John F. Mesick, Minister of Salem German Reformed Church. 93" x 95". Cotton materials in white with prints of red, green, and yellow. Red print double sawtooth border with feather quilting; feather quilting repeated in circles on the white background. Photograph courtesy of The State Museum of Pennsylvania.

2.17

2.18. Whig Rose, appliquéd quilt, Reformed, c. 1860, Boyertown, Berks County. Made by the Stauffer-Hankey family. 88" x 89". Cotton materials in white with red, green, orange, and blue. Flower and leaf quilting. The four-block motif is typical of mid-century Pennsylvania-German quilts. Collection of Holly Green; photograph by Ken White.

The plain geometric patch had returned to quilting favor.

If any quilt design remained a staple of thrift and warmth and rarely had any religious connotation or even decorative association, it was the one-, two-, and four-patch (figures 3.58 and 3.59). But the geometric patch, which has its roots in the high-style Indian palampore, was not always plain. The artistry of the Nine-Patch sometimes snowballed into a meaningful symmetry (figures 2.27, 2.28, and 2.30) and, as in the case of the Kriebel quilt (figure 2.29), suggested the valley in which the

2.18

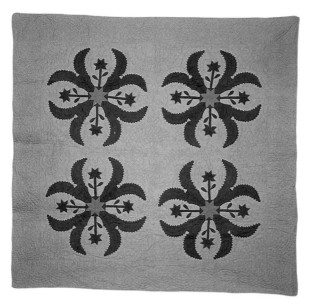

2.19

2.20

2.19. Lily (Cactus), pieced and appliquéd quilt, Lutheran, c. 1890, Earl Township, Berks County. Made by Mahella Rhodes Wolfgang. 85" x 82". Cotton materials in red, yellow, green, and a blue and white print. Pennsylvania-German women did not necessarily know that they were reviving Mary when they chose to piece or appliqué a lily quilt. But they did enjoy associating women with flowers and with the virtues linked by emblem books to the flower tradition. Collection of Nancy Roan; photograph by Ken White.

2.20. Detail, North Carolina Lily (Triple Tulip), pieced and appliquéd quilt, Mennonite, c. 1865, Line Lexington, Bucks County. Probably made by Maria Gehman Ruth. 85" square. Cotton materials in white, red, green, blue, and yellow. The lily, in art history, was the leading symbol of the young Virgin, a natural miracle. It was the source of the tulip design. The Pennsylvania Germans decorated just about everything with lilies. Collection of the Mennonite Heritage Center; photograph courtesy of John W. Munro, Harleysville, Pennsylvania.

2.21

2.21. Star, pieced quilt, Amish, 1938, Lancaster County. Maker unknown. 87" x 89$^1/_2$". Wool crepe materials in two shades of green, three of blue, maroon, pink, and purple. The construction is entirely of small diamonds. A vine and flower quilting pattern is worked in the border; elsewhere there is feather quilting. From mariners to ministers, celestial designs have always represented divine guidance. Anabaptists, the source of the Mennonites and Amish, responded strongly to the star, a symbol of their belief in the image of shadow and light. Collection of Dr. and Mrs. Donald M. Herr; photograph by Ken White.

2.22. Star, pieced quilt, Dutch Reformed, c. 1880, Churchville, Bucks County. Made by Adrianna Kroesen. 104" x 106". Cotton materials of white with prints of red, blue, and yellow. The construction is of small diamonds. The star is surrounded by sunbursts and the pattern is often referred to as the Star of Bethlehem. The star satisfied the churchly quilter as much as the sectarian. It was the most popular quilt image in central Pennsylvania. Photograph courtesy of the Mercer Museum of the Bucks County Historical Society.

2.23. Star (Postage Stamp), pieced quilt, Mennonite, c. 1880, locale unknown. Maker unknown. 77" square. Cotton materials in red, green, yellow, pink, gray, brown and prints of blue and white. The construction is of small square patches. The interior diamond resembles the design usually referred to as Trip Around the World. Photograph courtesy of M. Finkel and Daughter, Inc.

2.22

2.23

2.24. Variable Star, pieced pillow-sham, Mennonite, c. 1830, Sellersville, Bucks County. Maker unknown. Made for the Nase family. Dimensions unknown. Cotton materials in white with prints in blue and black, one identifiable as an English copperplate print. Some sectarians used the complex quilting techniques which made the star seem to sparkle. These quilters seem to be among those living in the large towns or mixed communities in mid-century. Collection of Mrs. William Highouse on loan to Mennonite Heritage Center photograph courtesy of John W. Munro, Harleysville, Pennsylvania.

2.25. Detail, Compass, appliquéd crib quilt, Mennonite, Manor Township, Lancaster County. Maker unknown. 40" x 39". Cotton materials in white with prints in two types of red. Quilting follows appliquéd design, helping to provide the allover effect of sunbursts. Appliquéd hearts form compass design. Mennonites sometimes utilized the less complicated red calico on white to create the illusion of a star within a sun. Collection of Dr. and Mrs. Donald M. Herr, photograph by Ken White.

2.26. Detail, Compass (Robbing Peter to Pay Paul), pieced quilt, Mennonite, c. 1890, Salford, Montgomery County. Made by Annie Schatz Clemens Lederach. Dimensions unknown. Cotton materials in red and black. This variation of the sun or compass design resembles the quilting motif often referred to as the wineglass pattern. Although the motif required curves difficult to create, it was nonetheless popular. Collection of Sandra Highouse on loan to Mennonite Heritage Center; photograph courtesy of John W. Munro, Harleysville, Pennsylvania.

2.25

2.27

2.27. Nine-Patch, pieced quilt, Old Mennonite, c. 1890, Colebrookdale Township, Berks County. Made by members of the Bechtel family. 85" x 74". Cotton materials in white with red, green, yellow, and blue patches. Binding print made about 1860. Crosshatch quilting. The plain geometric quilt, considered by some scholars to be derived from the Afro-American community in the South, returned to quilting favor at the time of the Centennial. One-, two-, three- and four-patch quilts, equipped for thrift and warmth, rarely had religious or even decorative associations. Collection of Holly Green; photograph by Ken White.

2.28. Nine-Patch, pieced quilt, Schwenkfelder, c. 1900, Worcester (Perkiomen Valley), Montgomery County. Made by members of the Allen Kriebel family. 77" x 79". Cotton materials. Cotton sateen print backing typical of Montgomery County. Crosshatch quilting; zigzag border quilting. Brown quilting thread is used. Though distilling emotion and distancing viewers from heavy didactic meaning which realistic images often reflect, goemetric forms can still convey vague, uplifting sensations or, as in the Kriebel quilt, simply the valley in which the family lived. Collection of Nancy Roan; photograph by Ken White.

2.26

2.28

2.29

2.29. Reel and Oak Leaf, pieced and appliquéd quilt, Mennonite, c. 1870, York County. Maker unknown. 80" square. Cotton materials in red, green, and yellow. The pattern is framed with a double sawtooth border. The reel design made a good commemoration or presentation quilt. It allowed for inscriptions, crewelwork embroidery insets, and trapunto or stuffed work. A variation called Caesar's Crown (or simply Crown) draws attention to the literary reference to the crown of the kingdom, so well understood in the evangelical nineteenth century. Photograph courtesy of M. Finkel and Daughter, Inc.

2.30

2.30. One-Patch and Nine-Patch, pieced quilt, Moravian by donor, c. 1840 Bethlehem, Lehigh County. Maker unknown. Quilted by Mary C. Schweitzer for the Harke family. 78" x 80". Cotton materials in prints of orange, green, red, tan, and brown. Wide and narrow borders of two brown prints. The lining is in two wide panels of two different dotted fabrics. Simple quilting. The Nine-Patch was popular among the middle-conservative groups—some Mennonites, the Schwenkfelders, the Moravians, and some Refored. As an artistic expression, it was less typical of Amish and Lutheran quilters. Collection of the Moravian Museum and Tours, Bethlehem, Pennsylvania; photograph by Ken White.

2.31. Appliquéd bedcover top, Moravian, 1861, locale unknown. Quilt made by S. Agnes Kummer. Patches made by Sarah Hinchliffe. Made for Alice Pierce, Kummer's niece. 100" x 68". Cotton materials of twelve different prints, one of which can be identified as a wood block print. Flower and Bow-Tie designs circle the central medallion and form a border. The original patches were made about 1840, the quilt was made in 1861, and the appliqué was done by Fanny Pierce in the 1920s. Collection of the Moravian Museum and Tours, Bethlehem, Pennsylvania; photograph by Ken White.

family lived. Quilt scholar Nancy Roan has traced the popularity of the Nine-Patch from lower Lehigh County through northern to middle Montgomery County. Mennonite, Schwenkfelder, Moravian, and Reformed quilters liked the design, which also flourished in central Pennsylvania among Reformed Church women. Small patches arranged in diagonal lines and called "Irish Chain" were popular with Mennonites (figure 2 32). The same small patches, often arranged by Mennonites and Schwenkfelders in more showy diamond like dark and light bands, took on the names "Trip Around the World" and "Rainbow" (figure 2.33). When Mennonites actually used the diamond instead of the square patches and rolled them, the pattern became "Ocean Waves" (figure 2.34).

Among other small, complex, geometric designs was the illusionary Tumbling Blocks and Baby Blocks (figures 2.36 and 3.74). Although Lutheran and Reformed women worked intricate geometric variations (figures 2.35 and 2.37), Schwenkfelders, and even more particularly Mennonites, depended on geometry to stretch an artistic vocabulary limited by their theology. Lutherans used the typically American strip sewing technique called "Log Cabin," but the Mennonites needed abstraction at least until the last quarter of the nineteenth century

2.31

47

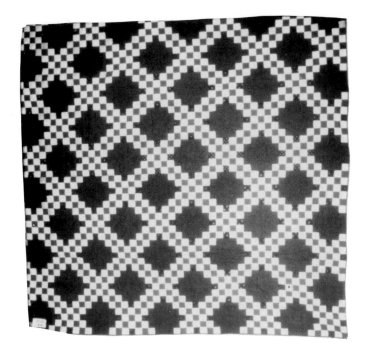

2.32

2.32. Detail, Double Irish Chain, pieced quilt, Mennonite, c. 1860-90, locale unknown. Made by Mary Overholt Loux Hunsberger. Dimensions unknown. Cotton materials in red, white, and black. Small patches organized in diagonal lines describe the Irish Chain pattern. It was restrained and popular with Mennonites. Collection of Mr. and Mrs. Ted Moyer on loan to the Mennonite Heritage Center; photograph courtesy of John W. Munro, Harleysville Pennsylvania.

2.33

2.33. Trip Around the World, pieced quilt, Mennonite, c. 1870, locale unknown. Maker unknown. Cotton materials in yellow, blue, red, and green. When small patches were arranged in elaborate diamond-like dark and light bands, they received the secular name "Trip Around the World." The technique of setting a square like a diamond is also used in the Rainbow pattern. It is different from Rising Star and Sunburst designs which are formed by true diamond templates. Collection of Mr. and Mrs. John L. Krupp on loan to Mennonite Heritage Center; photograph courtesy of John W. Munro, Harleysville, Pennsylvania.

2.34. Ocean Waves, pieced quilt, Mennonite, c. 1900, locale unknown. Maker unknown. Approximately 72" x 80". Cotton materials in prints of pink, red, yellow, and green. Diamond template construction. Narrow pink and green outer borders. When Mennonites chose small diamond patches instead of square ones and skewed them to roll as they were sewn, the image they presented of waves inspired the title of this design. Photograph courtesy of M. Finkel and Daughter, Inc.

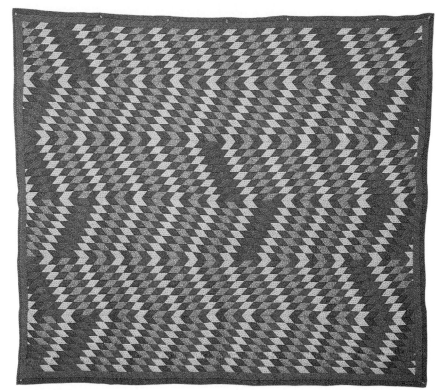

2.34

2.35. Wild Goose Chase Variation, pieced quilt, Lutheran, Bucks County. Maker unknown. 91" x 88". Cotton materials in orange, dark green, maroon, and white; the border is a striped print. Simple quilting. Collection of Mr. and Mrs. Howard Schanely; photograph by Ken White.

2.35

49

2.36. Pieced quilt, Mennonite, c. 1880, Hill Township, Bucks County. Made by members of the Enos B. Loux family. Dimensions unknown. Cotton materials in prints of brown with red, blue, pink, yellow, and white patches. Such geometric patterns as are found in this quilt—Tumbling Blocks, Baby Blocks, and Stairsteps—are included in the design category now called "quilts of illusion." Collection of Irene L. Bishop on loan to Mennonite Heritage Center; photograph courtesy of John W. Munro, Harleysville, Pennsylvania.

2.36

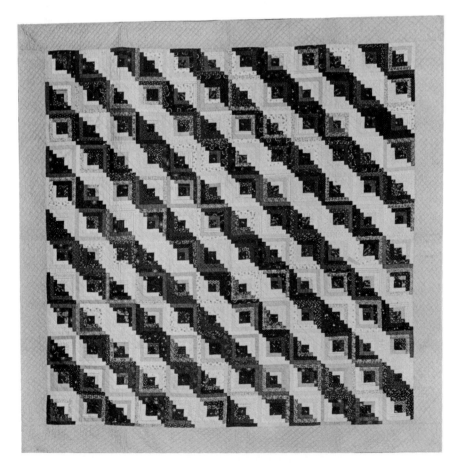

2.37. Log Cabin (Straight Furrow), pieced quilt, Reformed, c. 1890, Berks County. Made by members of the Darrah family. 91" square. Cotton materials in prints and stripes of brown, blue, maroon, tan, and white strips. Crosshatch quilting. Collection of Holly Green; photograph by Ken White.

2.38. Log Cabin (Pinwheel), pieced quilt, c. 1870, locale unknown. Maker unknown. 75" x 70". Wool materials in brown, red, blue, white, and yellow strips. Border is maroon with cable quilting. Abstract designs adhere to the twentieth-century delight with pure line, form, and color. But, since Amish spirituality was expressed in every job and gesture of every day, this Pinwheel or Windmill Blades motif was at least a sign of the joy of God's gift of creation. Collection of Mr. and Mrs. John B. Schorsch photograph by Ken White.

2.37

2.38

(figures 3.77 and 3.78). Like country Quakers, Mennonites felt more comfortable with the abstraction of a windblade (pinwheel) or pineapple (figure 2.38) than with an actual representation of one. Mennonites also coordinated Log Cabin strips in a semblance of Courthouse Steps (figure 2.39) Mennonites remained as suspicious of the power of realistic sketches and the fear of the Old Testament

2.39

2.39. Log Cabin (Courthouse Steps), pieced quilt, Mennonite, 1886, locale unknown. Made by Sally Grater Landis. Dimensions unknown. Cotton materials in brown, red, yellow, white, blue, and gray strips. Many Mennonites, planning abstract quilt patterns, remained suspicious of the power of realistic renderings. Like the Amish, many of them still observe the Old Testament prohibition against images. Collection of Mr. and Mrs. John Landis on loan to Mennonite Heritage Center; photograph courtesy of John W. Munro, Harleysville, Pennsylvania.

2.40

2.40. Bars, pieced quilt, Amish, c. 1890, Lancaster County. Maker unknown. 82" square. Wool crepe materials in red, blue, purple, and pink. The wide purple border is edged in blue. Simple quilting. An important function of quiltmaking for the Amish was the symbolic participation in the Reformation spirit. As theological, political, and social outsiders in Pennsylvania, the Amish viewed themselves metaphorically as being behind bars. If the name of this quilt suggests anything, it is protection. Photograph courtesy of M. Finkel and Daughter, Inc.

2.41. Diamond in a Square, pieced quilt, Amish, c. 1900, Lancaster County. Maker unknown. 78" square. Wool materials in purple, red, and green. The wide green border is edged in red. A key to this very special design can be found in Jenner's popular emblem book published in the seventeenth century. One emblem shows two frames—a diamond and a square—and explains that they are meant to fit one into the other the way man and God are meant to fit together. Photograph courtesy of M. Finkel and Daughter, Inc.

prohibition against images as Lutherans remained accepting of "the inevitability of imagery."[32] Time, however, has erased some of the limits on sectarian theology and on sectarian quilts.

For quilters generally there were all sorts of Log Cabin variations and almost as many names for any one design as quilters and writers could conjure. The American magazines *Ladies' Home Journal, Arthur's, Peterson's, Good Housekeeping, American Agriculturist*, and *National Stockman and Farmer* popularized the new pattern names. Ladies Art Company, the business of a German immigrant family, published over five hundred names by 1928. By the twentieth century the batting (cotton filler) wrappers used by Stearns and Foster's Mountain Mist Company circulated new and old pattern names.[33] The new labels symbolized interest in America's ancestry, America's simplicity, and America's dignity. The pattern name "Grandmother's Flower Garden" suddenly emerged as fashionable and arty quilting terminology at the same time that the term "Grandfather's Clock" (rather than the more formal "tall case clock") emerged as a reference to American respectability in the equally functional decorative arts.

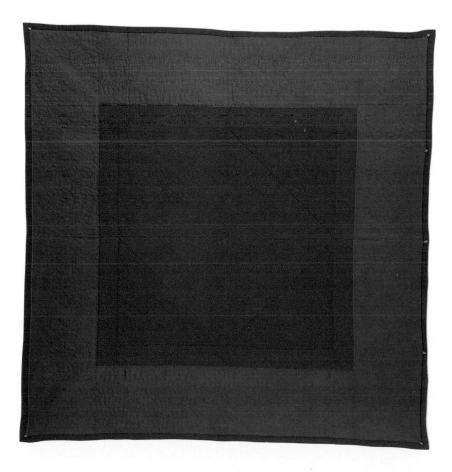

2.41

Finally, with the nineteenth-century Amish we come to one of the most distinct sects and some of the most abstract and simple pieced designs in the realm of Pennsylvania-German quilting. Quilt motif patches represent this group as standing outside the bars of tradition (figure 2.40) while living, like their diamond in a square, among insiders (figure 2.41). Understanding Amish signs gives us what Ricky Clark describes in the Oral Traditions Quilt Project as "a heady experience." An important function of quiltmaking generally was this symbolic participation in the Reformation spirit.

Today we can look at nineteenth-century Germanic taste, notice the natural motifs of the churchly set and the linear coolness of the sectarians and, if we were spiritually alert, perceive that for them, as for us, sackcloth and ashes are more than textiles and pollution. We can hope we have not imposed on these quilters of the past by unfolding their quilts and examining what is inside. But, if Annie Curd's words in *Good Housekeeping* in 1888 are correct, we have already imposed on the privacy of this functional memorial to women. As Annie said, a quilt "will seem like the face of a familiar friend, and will bring up a whole host of memories . . . too sacred for us to intrude upon." Eventually, as Margaret Miles writes in *Image as Insight*, "both verbal and visual texts must be used to illuminate, to correct, and to supplement the impression we get from each." Our lives, as she says, are "formed, informed, and supported by words and images."[34]

3. A Gallery of Pennsylvania-German Quilts

ORAL INTERVIEWS HAVE HELPED to provide over 6000 names for Pennsylvania-German quilt designs. Yet oral interviews, like the one with Ivy Kemp Yost of Berks County who claimed that for generations "we never knew [quilt] designs by names," provide a reason for not depending too completely on the literary aspect of objects and images.[1] And Mrs. Yost's sweeping aside of pattern names is also a caution to those using the oral interview as their only source of information about the quilting tradition.

But in order to address the subject of quilt designs, we do need to do some sort of naming. This chapter has been built on a small and arbitrary language bridge of nine logical quilt design categories—baskets; trees, hearts, lilies, roses, stars, compasses, reels, and angular geometrics. Wherever possible, however, the romantic, commercial, and religious pattern names are included in the captions. The literature of titles can certainly focus on the region or particular group of people to which an image may belong as well as on the meaning an image might possibly convey. Conclusions may always be debatable, but with titles such as "Job's Tears," "Morning Star," "Crown of Thorns," "Joseph's Coat," "Delectable Mountains," "Jacob's Ladder," and even "Diamond," it is reasonable to assume that quilters were aware, at some level, of their inherited religious traditions and communicated them. These titles function in much the same way as Robert Fludd's large "eye of the imagination" was supposed to function in the seventeenth century. Not coincidentally, this eye was drawn as if it were hidden in the center of the forehead, implying that images and designs emanated from the mind before craftsmen's hands could discharge them. Even then they believed that the most powerful way to send a message and to have it remembered was through design.[2]

Quilt images, as well as design names, range from the most identifiable and natural to the least identifiable and abstract. Realistic designs are associated with the structural technique of appliqué, which again is a stitching on top of the cloth instead of as part of it. Trees, fruit, birds, hearts, and roses mostly depended on the working of curves, a difficult task which invoked the professional and "fancy quilt" status. "Fancy" could mean many things. It could mean that the quilt was derived from prints and other high-style or literate sources and was motivated by aesthetic or fashionable impulses rather than practical ones. "Fancy" is currently being considered in light of Anglo-American traditions as opposed to Afro-American traditions present in American plantation society. "Fancy" could also mean that the quilter was capable of working ten to twelve stitches to the inch or that the quilter chose red and green instead of brown and tan. And, finally, "fancy" could mean accepting the churchly taste for traditional image reinforcement of the good without the typical nineteenth-century fears of being associated with the Roman Church or the occult.

The plain quilt, as opposed to the fancy quilt, is considered by some to be more "painterly." " Some say that the pieced quilt is more American, more Pennsylvania- German, and more sectarian. Statistics from the sampling in this book underline these assumptions. Only thirty of the 130 quilts pictured in these chapters have been appliquéd. Twenty-eight were pieced and appliquéd. Seventy-two, or over twice the number in either of the previous categories, were pure pieced work. Four times as many pieced quilts as appliquéd or fancy quilts were positively identified in Chapter 2 as Pennsylvania German. And, although the churchly Germans were free to piece and appliqué, the sectarians were more compelled in the pieced and abstract direction. More than one-third of the illustrations in Chapter 3 are plain and generally associated with sectarian quilters.

Pennsylvania Germans, like quilters and needleworkers generally, began their work with wools. Wool was the important eighteenth-century textile commodity. Sectarian quilters like the Amish, however, were the only ones still favoring wool in the twentieth century. The geometric quilts of other groups sometimes combined woolen fabrics with those of other materials (figures 3.58 and 3.59). With the invention of cotton-picking machines, copperplate and roller printing devices, and new dye techniques being applied also to thread manufacture (aniline dyes emerging in 1857), printed fabrics began to appear in quantity in quilts. Florals, plaids, stripes, and dots were favored by all except the Amish (figures 3.67 and 3.68). Silk, occasionally found as part of eighteenth-century textiles, was mass produced in 1880 and showed up in Log Cabin pieced quilts (figure 3.80), in Wild Goose Chase designs (figure 3.73), and in the fashionable Victorian crazy quilts. Technology can thus help to date the Pennsylvania-German silk quilts as having developed between 1880 and 1920, the pattern which incorporated the silk being of the pieced and geometric sort.

The size of a quilt varied less than one might guess. Of the quilts examined for this book two-thirds were square or nearly square. Almost half the quilts ranged between seventy and eighty-eight inches. Eleven quilts were over a hundred inches. Four quilts were under forty inches. In this sampling the forty-inch or crib-size is even more rare than the oversized quilt.

One of the earliest dated patterns made in America has been described as the Feathered Star, which American writer Mrs. Hall recorded as having been done at least as early as 1771. The earliest Pennsylvania-German quilt pattern shown in this book is the repeat Variable Star (figure 2.13) made by a Moravian and dated 1830. The Star is followed by the Reel and Orange Peel (sometimes called a crown). Two are shown here, a Lutheran one dated 1843 and a Moravian one dated 1849. Beside the Star and the Reel, the Nine-Patch, Compass, and Lily were among the designs which appeared in the 1840s and continued in popularity through the 1920s. The Heart and Fruit Branch also emerged in the 1840s, but were never truly popular among the Germans as a group.

Colors had their own effect, both on the eye and the mind. Deep blue, deep crimson, olive green, and yellow were eighteenth-century English linsey-woolsey colors popular again with the Amish after 1900. The nineteenth century was generally filled with bright reds, greens, yellows, and pinks. Color was an important element in the small piecing designs of the Star, Rainbow, Trip Around the World (which Averil Colby calls "frame quilts"), and the geometric quilts of illusion. Yellow-orange background colors have been important to the identification of Lancaster and Dauphin eagle quilts. Of course to the Amish, with their limited fabric designs, color was crucial. And ultimately around the color red the churchly and sectarian conflict is emblazoned. "Scripture quilts," made by the churchly groups (whether they were Pennsylvania-German or Anglo-American) and destined for the pastors or for the church itself, are identified quickly by pieced solid-color fabrics of bright red and pure white. Red was the color of martyrs, of sacrifice, of Jesus. But to the Mennonites the color red signified the evil of the harlot. It was a color they tried to avoid at all costs.

Like color and fabric designs, the quilting stitch has a history of its own. Though popular quilt names were not derived from it, it was the stitch, holding the three layers of fabric together, that created the first quilt designs.[3] From what S. F. A. Caulfield and Blanche Saward wrote in 1882 in their *Dictionary of Needlework*, the independent stitching patterns were, like pieced work, originally geometric. As Caulfield and Saward said, ". . . the Runnings [were] . . . made diagonally, so as to form a pattern of diamonds, squares or octagons." The diamond shape was called "Gamboised."

But stitched quilting patterns, like fabric design and color, could be plain or could be fancy. By arranging quilting stitches into three categories divided according to function, quilt scholar Jonathan Holstein clarified how they arrived at being plain or fancy. In the first category, the stitching followed the fabric patches, and, if they were fancy, the stitching was fancy. In the second, the stitching created its own independent pattern and was the creative agent on empty backgrounds, borders, corners, and sometimes in central areas such as the large diamond or square centers of the Amish quilts. The most popular quilting motif in the second category was the feather pattern. Sometimes it appeared thin and sometimes wide. Sometimes it was undulating and sometimes circular like a wreath. And sometimes it was a series of single designs called "Princess Feather" or a set of triple designs called "Prince of Wales." Other independent patterns included flowers, fruits, hearts, branches, vines, the cable, lozenge, and swag and tassel.

In the third and often least varied category there were the fillers, the stitches which tied down the three layers of fabric. The fillers alternated between the diagonal, the double diagonals, and the simple cross-hatch stitches. These straight lines were the preferred methods of tacking down the three layers, even though circular and scroll designs were the most efficient in keeping the wadding secure.

But whether it was in the mechanics of joining materials, choosing colors, stitching within a given space, or being churchly or sectarian, the fancy quilting process, as well as much that we call "pieced," implied the necessity of having time, experience, and a willingness to work for adornment. It required an optimistic and worldly attitude towards beauty or a very good explanation in defence of beauty, one acceptable to an essentially religious community. Very little quilting time was needed technically to meet the practical condition of warmth in the period when Pennsylvania-German quilting flourished. A great deal more time, however, was needed to turn the utilitarian quilt into an aesthetically and spiritually satisfying experience.

Baskets

PENNSYLVANIA-GERMAN BASKET MOTIFS usually consist of pieces of triangular fabric pieced together to form blocks or squares. The angles, however they are cut, stir the eye and the mind. Contrasting colors and prints create more interest in triangular geometry than in less angular motifs. Rarely is a totally curved, naturalistic appliquéd basket design (frequently found on Maryland quilts) considered of Pennsylvania-German origin.

Often what visually appears as a one-piece background cloth may be instead single blocks set on point (figure 3.1). The repeat patterns also set on point are sometimes enhanced by what Mennonites use and call the sashing and square separations (figure 3.2). Since the Amish tend to be sparing with any realistic design, they alternated basket motif blocks, if they were tempted to use them, with solid squares of fabric.

A basket may include a pieced or appliquéd top handle. If a seeming basket includes only side handles, it is in actuality a pot. Curved handles require appliqué, as do the flowers sometimes found in the baskets and pots.

Sometimes the basket, like the potted Triple Lily design, is arranged so that the flowers face only one way (figure 3.18). Sometimes, however, the floral design is turned towards the center of the quilt, radiating away from three of the four borders (figure 3.15). Such juxtapositions provide even more visual stimulation than those in which flowers are all sitting upright.

3.1

3.1. Basket, pieced and appliquéd crib quilt, Mennonite, c. 1898, Doylestown, Bucks County. Made by Lydia Nice Detweiler for Paul Detweiler. 30¹/₂" square. Cotton. Each green and white print basket is pieced in a block of white and green print set on point. The rounded basket handle is appliquéd, as all rounded forms are, a more difficult task than a pieced handle as in figure 3.3. Large triangles, which form the inner quilt edge, are pieced around the white squares and face inward, decoratively. Two straight outer borders, one of the white print and one of the green, frame the quilt. The backing is in blue. Simple quilting holds the layers together. Courtesy Mennonite Heritage Center.

60

3.2

3.2. Basket, pieced and appliquéd quilt, c. 1910, locale unknown. Maker unknown. 83" square. Cotton. The basic block design, composed of red and dark-green triangles pieced together with a white and blue printed fabric, makes a striking quilt. The small triangles and expert piecing technique give this quilt a smoother and more sophisticated effect than that achieved in figure 3.1. Each basket includes a sprouting flower which is appliquéd, as is the handle. The squares, set as diamonds, maintain unity as well as separateness through the use of typical Mennonite sashing and square pieces. Partial feathered wreath quilting can be found in the triangles edging the four borders. Collection of Robert L. Schaeffer, Jr., in Permanent Collection, Franklin and Marshall College; photograph by Ken White.

3.3

3.3. Basket, pieced quilt, c. 1920, locale unknown. Maker unknown. 75" x 76". Cotton. Prints of five different blue designs and two pink and blue fabrics create twenty-five filled basket blocks. Each basket has a pieced sawtooth handle rather than the appliquéd handle seen in figures 3.1 and 3.2. The three triangles placed in the center of each basket are pieced in a print different from the one used to create the handle and the basket. They represent the fullness of the basket. The choice of background fabric, a white and blue-dotted print, creates a subtle sashing as opposed to the striking contrasts in figure 3.2. The large triangular pieces of fabric that make up the turned-in sawtooth border are ornamented with what would be a full-circle feathered wreath with a crosshatched or latticework center. Cable quilting edges the outer border. Collection of Robert L. Schaeffer, Jr., in Permanent Collection, Franklin and Marshall College; photograph by Ken White.

62

Trees and Boughs of Fruit

ALTHOUGH THE REPERTOIRE of tree patterns includes the geometric or triangle-patch tree (which is very similar in piecing construction to the basket motif), it is the more realistic tree and its accompanying fruit or branches of fruit which concern us here. Essentially these trees and their fruits are difficult appliquéd forms, "fancywork" which took extra time and skill. The appliquéd tree was a symbolic reminder to churchly Germans of the fullness of marriage, the bride and groom being reminiscent of the church community committing itself to the Lord. With such spiritual connotations, it was not unusual for trees to be included on bridal quilts.

Functionally, appliqué creates problems. It does not usually offer the quilter the smooth surface of a pieced design. A curved shape cannot immediately be joined to other fabric by a straight seam. It requires that margins be basted, then sewn to the background with small hemming stitches, and finally ornamented with a decorative top stitch. Despite the technical complexity of fancy tree, fruit and bird motifs on appliquéd quilts, most pieced quilts are a constant reminder that plain quilts are not necessarily simple.

3.4

3.4. Tree of Knowledge, appliquéd bridal quilt, c. 1860, locale unknown. Maker unknown. 94" x 72". Cotton. The colors are white with yellow-green tree trunks and branches to which are attached orange and red fruit. The colored fabrics are printed. Two types of cording are used. Each of the designs is outline quilted. The diagonal line or row which forms a lattice is known as crosshatching and is used here as filler quilting. Structurally, the appliquéd tree design is difficult to cut and stitch because creating the fruit involves forming a complicated curve. The tree includes two kinds of fruit and represents the Tree of Knowledge in the earthly garden as opposed to the Tree of Life, a symbol of the heavenly garden (see figure 2.12). Private collection; photograph by Ken White.

3.5. Appliquéd and pieced signature quilt, dated 1850, Milton, Union County. Maker unknown. 97" x 101". This quilt is a memorial to Lila Goodrich Lerch, granddaughter of the Rev. William Goodrich and Elizabeth Straute Goodrich. All the leaves are green; the flowers and grapes, red. One butterfly is appliquéd in orange. The motifs suggest spring, the time of birth and symbol of rebirth, and are appropriate for a memorial quilt. The designs, intricately appliquéd to white blocks, brilliantly conceal signatures. The names seem almost to grow out of the branches. The border is a series of single, hooked green branches of flowers and leaves appliquéd to half blocks which were then pieced to the other blocks. Names are sewn in these half blocks, too. Simple quilting appears across the appliquéd blocks, and crosshatch quilting fills in the white areas connecting the blocks. The quilting stitches, delicately close, measure twelve stitches to the inch. Cable quilting, six-rows wide, covers the white border.

3.5

3.6

Among the names found on this quilt, all of them of people from Milton, Pennsylvania, include Catherine, Martha, and Kate Strine; Elizabeth Wierline; Christiana Trout; Sarah Shoemaker; Kate G. Swenk; and Maria E. Schmoyer. Courtesy Historical Society of Berks County.

3.6. Detail, appliquéd album quilt, c. 1850, southern Lancaster County. Maker unknown. 87" x 88". Cotton. Several squares contain red, purple, and some green grapes with green leaves and wide green stems and slender green tendrils. The grape design is particularly imaginative and

seems to float even though there are almost imperceptibly embroidered stems. The quilting follows the appliquéd design. Although this quilt was probably made by a group of quilters, it is referred to as an album quilt because there are no signatures. Collection of Dr. and Mrs. Donald M. Herr; photograph by Ken White.

3.7

3.7. Fig and Leaf, appliquéd quilt, c. 1860, locale unknown. Maker unknown. 78" square. Cotton. An extraordinary array of leaves – almost a botanical assortment – ornament this quilt in red and green printed fabric. The large central scalloped design, created by a bold appliquéd and undulating red feathered vine, is itself surrounded by a diamond shape formed from leafed branches carrying stars with trapunto centers and red leaves at each point. The entire design is appliquéd to a white block structurally pieced and set on point. An appliquéd branch of figs and leaves creates an outer square which is then connected to the inner diamond by diagonal branches and red and green leaves. The fig design, unusual for a quilt, has equally unusual blue stems. Perhaps it is not coincidental that the quilt resembles the New Testament description of "a fig tree having leaves . . . nothing but leaves" (Mark 11:13). The quilt has a border of undulating appliquéd vines with leaf designs rather than the feathered pattern of the central vine. A similar vine in each corner surrounds a green and red sun design. Quilting follows the appliquéd designs. Quilting patterns covering the white ground include circles, lozenges, tulips, and three-inch-diameter feather circles. Crosshatching fills the white panels that surround the diamond-like center design. Private collection; photograph by Ken White.

3.8. Branch and Bird, appliquéd panel, probably Lutheran or Reformed, c. 1900, central or northern Pennsylvania. Maker unknown. 24" x 23". Cotton. This simple panel of bright yellow is a rather untypical interpretation of the German mystic's two birds drinking from the spiritual tulip/lily. It is shocking in its color, its contrast, and its fluid design. The birds are red; the tree form is dark green. The two intertwining crescents with leaf tips supporting the flower are a yellow-orange. Each piece is appliquéd onto the bright yellow background. Although unquilted, the panel is a little masterpiece. Collection of Germantown Historical Society; photograph by Ken White.

3.8

Hearts

NOT MANY HEARTS exist as central motifs in the Pennsylvania-German quilt tradition. Like birds, hearts are found in medieval iconography as well as in the sophisticated English needlework tradition. Because of the motif's round, over-heavy top and pointed bottom, it could never be part of the pieced quilt vocabulary. But, even when the heart was used in appliqué, it was often as part of the formation of another motif, as in the compass seen in figure 3.11. In effect, the heart, like the symbols of nineteenth-century fraternal organizations, had a masked existence in quilts. Though ministers and teachers painted the heart freely on their fraktur, incorporating it as a symbol with the flower in the garden, quilters most often designed hearts in graceful but hard-to-see white-on-white quilting stitches, worked independently of any appliquéd motifs.

3.9. Pieced and appliquéd signature quilt, Mennonite, dated 1897, Bally, Berks County. Made by Mary Gehman Kriebel and friends. Cotton. At one end of this quilt is a green heart set against a yellow diamond. At the opposite end is a yellow star against a green square. These yellow and green patches are surrounded by geometric patterns—among them Chimney Sweep, Variable Star, Triple Lily, Fan, Nine-Patch, Four T, Basket, Cross, and Bars—each block separated by black sashing and yellow squares. In addition to green and yellow fabrics, brown, rust, red, pink, gray, light blue, and white fabrics are used. The quilt contains sixty-one blocks, each of which was worked by a friend of Mary Gehman Kriebel's. Each block bears the respective quilter's name, printed by Mary's cousin, Daniel G. Gehman, who added his own name and the date to the top of the quilt. The blocks were assembled by Mary Gehman Kriebel. Among the names printed are Sarah Gross, Bertha B. Good, Lizzie Beidler, Mary Ann B. Gehman, Emme Kolb, Susanna L. Musser, and Elizabeth Weber. One modern term for this assembledge of different blocks is a "friendship quilt." Collection of Lydia G. Kriebel on loan to Mennonite Heritage Center; photograph by John W. Munro, Harleysville, Pennsylvania.

3.9

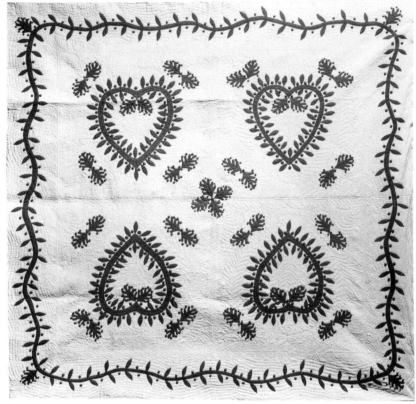

3.10

3.10. Hearts, appliquéd quilt, c. 1850, locale unknown. Maker unknown. 87" x 88". Cotton. The bleached white background fabric, a plain weave of eighty warps to the inch, is appliquéd with blue vines and hearts and with red berries done in the stuffed or trapunto style. These designs required skill and diligence to provide the intricate cutting and sewing of lozenge-shaped leaves, of pairs of fern-like leaves, and of numerous berries which surround each pair of fern-like leaves. Leaves and berries are also attached to the border vine. The white, seemingly solid, background is actually four squares pieced together and joined to a white border. Most appliquéd quilts are structurally pieced in this manner. The reverse is pieced in three panels. Feather pattern quilting surrounds the hearts. A straight feather design is quilted inside the hearts. Quilting in a leaf design covers the white background. The border is quilted in a wave pattern. Courtesy Philadelphia Museum of Art; Titus C. Geesey Collection.

3.11. Heart and Compass (Sunflower), pieced and appliquéd quilt, c. 1840-80, locale unknown. Maker unknown. 88$\frac{1}{2}$" x 78". Cotton. The bleached white background is pieced from thirty blocks. Compass, heart, and tulip motifs are appliquéd in red, green, and yellow prints. The vine is appliquéd in brown; the birds, in green and brown. The bird, undulating vine, and stylized flower on the border suggest the hand of an expert quilter. Tulip and leaf pattern quilting covers the background between the appliqué designs. Courtesy Philadelphia Museum of Art; Titus C. Geesey Collection.

3.11

3.12. Heart and Rose, pieced and appliquéd quilt, c. 1870, Sinking Springs (near Reading), Berks County. Maker unknown. 78" x 82". Cotton. This white pieced-block quilt is dependent for its beauty on the appliqué of roses and hearts and the strong color repeats of red and green. These bold repeat motifs are a contrast to the delicate and varied sets of patterns seen in figure 3.5. They resemble more the arrangement of motifs in figure 3.11. The white four-paneled border is ornamented by an appliquéd vine which carries the leaves and rosebuds in a tight arrangement. Although one expects to find the vine green and the rosebud red, it is unique to find that these leaves and bud calyxes are a light blue. The quilting follows the pattern across the blocks. A quilting pattern of leaves and flowers is also apparent on the main body of the quilt. The border appliqué includes quilting which follows it and leaf designs which branch out independently. Photograph courtesy Historical Society of Berks County.

3.13. Hearts (Heart and Hex), pieced and appliquéd quilt top, c. 1830, Germantown, stamped "Mary C. Smith". 95" x 84". Cotton. The white fabric, actually a fine muslin similar to the textile originally made in India, is composed of white blocks appliquéd with a dark blue and white dotted print in the shape of ten-pointed sunbursts. Hearts are attached to the points. A leafed flower extends from four of the hearts on each of the circular patterns. The very elaborate design forming the border consists of thick undulating vines with rose or dahlia blossoms and berries and leaves. The top is unquilted. Collection of Germantown Historical Society; photograph by Ken White.

3.12

3.13

Lilies or Tulips

THE LILY OR TULIP, a symbol of purity and, hence, the Virgin, and the attribute of the Archangel Gabriel, was also a versatile sewing motif. It was pieced and appliquéd much like the more geometric basket design. The arrangement was often as a single flower, as shown in figures 3.14 and 3.16. Sometimes it was as a triple blossom on a single stem, as in figures 3.15 and 3.18. The flower could be held by a stem or a twig, and it could also be potted. When it was designed in a reel-type variation, the flower was often referred to as a cactus (figure 3.19). Reflecting the floral imagery of the Bible, central and eastern Pennsylvania quilters enjoyed including the lily or tulip with the rose. Their repeat designs of a floral wreath often incorporated both flowers. As a rule, the Amish avoided the lily, both because it was a naturalistic design and because it required appliquéd stems and, when pots were used, appliquéd handles. As Rachel and Kenneth Pellman observe in *The World of Amish Quilts*, the lily was considered too much "a showy pattern" for Amish women.

3.14. Detail, Lily, appliquéd quilt, c. 1900, locale unknown. Maker unknown. 66" x 73". Cotton. On the white background the quilter appliquéd red and yellow fabric for the flowers and fugitive (faded) green fabric for the stems. One set of quilting stitches follows the appliquéd design. A second, simple set is used as a filler. The quilt is beautiful in its simplicity. Private collection; photograph by Ken White.

3.14

72

3.15. North Carolina Lily (Triple Tulip), pieced and appliquéd quilt, Mennonite, c. 1865, Bucks or Montgomery County. Made by Maria Gehman Ruth for the Noah Ruth family. 85" square. Cotton. The flowers are red with green calyxes, stems, and leaves. Simultaneously separating and tying together the floral blocks, the sashing is light blue with yellow squares. The border pattern is composed of red squares set as diamonds and lily heads extending from the four edges of the quilt. Collection of Mennonite Heritage Center; photograph by John W. Munro, Harleysville, Pennsylvania.

3.15

3.16

3.16. Detail, pieced and appliquéd album quilt, probably Mennonite, c. 1895, Lancaster County. Made by Lizzie Kulp Buck of Akron, Pennsylvania, for her daughter Bertha K. Shirk. 42" square. Cotton. The four designs—lily, flower, leaf, and reel—are made from dark-red, yellow, and green fabrics with one yellow and two different red prints. A typically Pennsylvania-German sectarian approach to appliqué is illustrated here, as "fancy work" (which Jeannette Lasansky in *Heart of Pennsylvania* defines as appliqué) has been employed to create a design that is almost too simple for the fancy sewing technique. This quilt is a reminder that what is plain can also be fancy. Mrs. Buck made two of these quilts, the second one for a second daughter. The quilting pattern she chose is a simple chevron design. Collection of Dr. and Mrs. Donald M. Herr; photograph by Ken White.

3.17. Triple Lily, appliquéd quilt, c. 1860, locale unknown. Maker unknown. 88" square. Cotton. The white background is appliquéd with prints of red, yellow, and green fabric in the shape of triple flowers. The border of flowers, leaves, and vines is less complicated than the undulating vine in figure 3.13, but very effective and appropriate to the simple statement of the triple lily. A quilted feather and flower design decorates the white background between the patterns. Crosshatch quilting helps to fill the other spaces. Collection of Robert L. Schaeffer, Jr., in Permanent Collection, Franklin and Marshall College; photograph by Ken White.

3.18. North Carolina Lily (Triple Tulip), pieced and appliquéd quilt, Schwenkfelder, c. 1880, Montgomery County. Made by Clarella Dresher Anders. 77" square. Cotton. Each of the white background blocks contains a pot with an appliquéd handle and a triple lily pieced and appliquéd in prints of red and green. The handles placed on the sides of the container rather than across the top identify it as a pot and not a basket. The pot form is made on the diagonal of the block. Note that the plant stems do not join the flower calyxes at the natural point and that the center flower in each pot does not meet the stem. As Nancy Roan observes, quilters were rarely concerned with botanical perfection. The quilting is in a simple latticework pattern. Collection of Mrs. Stephen Palmer, Jr.; photograph by Ken White.

3.19. Double Lily (Cactus), pieced and appliquéd quilt, c. 1880, locale unknown. Maker unknown. 72" x 78". Cotton. Red, green, and yellow printed fabrics are appliquéd to create each remarkable four-lily design as well as to develop the center potted flower and the small single flowers and stems. One of the more subtle aspects of these large patterns rests with the centers which form the four lilies. Unlike the major work on the quilt, which is appliqué, these centers are made up of diamonds pieced to form the central eight-pointed stars. After the four large white blocks were pieced together, the flowerpot and single flower twigs were delicately appliquéd to cover the white block seams. A wide print border frames the blocks and is simply quilted. Flower patterns are quilted in the corners. Collection of Robert L. Schaeffer, Jr., in Permanent Collection, Franklin and Marshall College; photograph by Ken White.

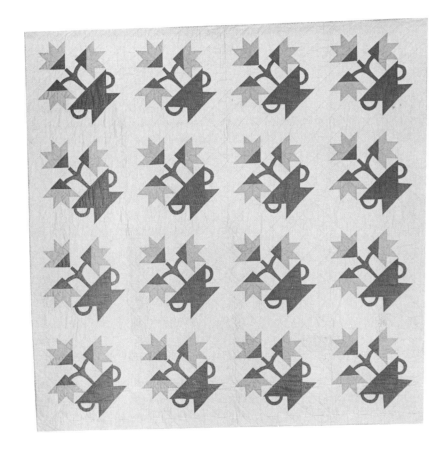

3.18

3.19

Roses

THE ROSE DESIGN REQUIRES APPLIQUÉ. It usually comes to us in two basic design forms—as part of a wreath or as a central motif with four branches giving it a squared appearance. In wreaths like those shown in figure 3.20, the design is achieved by joining a combination of tulips, buds, and leaves. Although the colors are usually consistent with nature, that is, in greens and reds, on occasion the entire project is creatively worked in shades of yellow, brown, and green-blue fabrics, as in figure 3.21. The rose wreath done in shades of pink and green prints is more likely to be found in a quilt which is both pieced and appliquéd. The greens and reds are usually employed in the pure appliquéd quilt.

The rose as a central square-type motif has been called the Whig Rose or the Rose of Sharon (a name known to the Pennsylvania-Germans as a garden plant and as a plant mentioned in the Old Testament Song of Solomon. In her books Jeannette Lasansky uses the labels "Rose of Sharon" and "Whig Rose" interchangeably. Phyllis Haders, on the other hand, distinguishes the two by maintaining that the Rose of Sharon supports four curving branches, as in figures 3.23 and 3.24, whereas the Whig Rose supports four very straight branches, as in figures 2.18 and 3.25. And Nancy Roan reminds us that both names are regional and, thus, correct. Under either name this slightly abstracted, less than naturalistic rose is without the visual heroic overtones of the rose wreath.

3.20. Detail, Rose Wreath, appliquéd quilt, c. 1860, locale unknown. Maker unknown. 75" x 88". Cotton. This white quilt is decorated with red roses stuffed in the trapunto style and with orange crewel wool embroidered centers. The roses are joined together by a wreath of green stems and leaves. Red buds and green leaves on a meandering green vine create the inner border. Quilting stitches follow the appliquéd elements; there is also simple filler quilting. In *The Romance of the Patchwork Quilt* (1935), Carrie Hall describes this design as the "President's Wreath," but the name is but one of many applied to the pattern. Private collection; photograph by Ken White.

3.21. Detail, Rose and Tulip Wreath, appliquéd signature quilt, Lutheran, dated October, 1881, Lebanon County. Made by Edna E. Meyer or Lizzie S. Herr. 91" x 89". Cotton. Brown roses and tulips are appliquéd to a tan print background. The roses have yellow centers. The calyx of each tulip, the leaves, and the stems which form the wreath are appliquéd in a blue-green fabric. The backing, of which one corner is shown, is in large panels of rusty brown and blue-green. The appliqué border consists of swags with simple flowers, a ram's horn form (easily mistaken for a tassel), and a small potted tulip. Quilting in leaf, heart, and star patterns surrounds the appliquéd border. The quilt contains the ink signatures of Edna E. Meyer on one corner, of Christina Herr and Sobina Herr on one quilted star, and of Lizzie S. Herr on another star. Lizzie S. Herr's initials— L.S.H.— are also appliquéd on the quilt. Note, however, that the middle initial was executed backwards. Collection of Mr. and Mrs. Victor L. Johnson; photograph by Ken White.

3.20

3.22. Rose and Bud, pieced and appliquéd quilt, c. 1860, locale unknown. Maker unknown. 102" x 104". Cotton. Each rose is composed of a red print with a yellow center, a pink print with red dots, and an outer red print. The elements are appliquéd on a white ground. The yellow rose centers are embroidered with a buttonhole stitch. Red buds with printed green calyxes, also buttonhole stitched, are set around each rose. Between these large floral repeats the quilter pieced green printed sashing and red and yellow printed squares. While they join the white blocks, which are set on point, they also visually separate and open out the designs. A border of white cotton is appliquéd with undulating vines in a green print different from the other greens on the quilt. The vines are ornamented with delicate red, green, and yellow leaves, the red and the green being solid-color fabrics. The fragility of the outside border design is in startling contrast with the visual solidity of the inner appliqués. Simple quilting follows the appliquéd design. The only independent quilting pattern is the corner flower sewn into each block. A simple crosshatch pattern covers the rest of the quilt. Collection of Mr. and Mrs. Victor L. Johnson; photograph by Ken White.

3.21

3.22

3.23

3.23. Rose of Sharon (Whig Rose), pieced and appliquéd quilt, c. 1860, locale unknown. Maker unknown. 81" x 84". Cotton. Prints in green, yellow, and red on a white blocked background are framed by two borders, one an outer undulating vine border with flowers and leaves and the other an interior sawtooth border design. Besides the two pattern names listed above, this design is also referred to in different regions as Spice Pink. Collection of Robert L. Schaeffer, Jr., in Permanent Collection, Franklin and Marshall College; photograph by Ken White.

3.24

3.24. Rose of Sharon (Whig Rose), appliquéd quilt, probably Reformed, c. 1870, locale unknown. Maker unknown. 90" x 91". Cotton. The white background with solid green, yellow, red, and red print fabrics is bordered by appliquéd swags and tassels, which add to the elegance of the quilt. Independent feather pattern quilting is interspersed with simple crosshatching across the background fabric. Collection of Robert L. Schaeffer, Jr., in Permanent Collection, Franklin and Marshall College; photograph by Ken White.

3.25

3.25. Whig Rose (Rose of Sharon), appliquéd quilt, probably Reformed, dated 1857, locale unknown. Made by "M. R." 80" x 92". Cotton. This white quilt is appliquéd with tulips and roses created from red prints and solid-yellow fabric. The stems, calyxes, and leaves on the outer vines are made from green fabric. The leaves on the central patterns are appliquéd in red as are the initials and the date positioned in two of the four corners. Arched vines intermingle with thin flower stems to create a pleasing and almost fence-like border on all four sides. The quilting is simple. The pattern name, Whig Rose, seems to refer to the central flower and possibly the smaller circular flowers on the branches. Invariably four tulip shapes sprout from the central rose to form a cross. The large alternating branches, which suggest another sort of cross, also extend from the central rose. The pattern has also been referred to as the Rose of Sharon, despite the fact that some writers think the Whig Rose has straight stems and the Rose of Sharon, curved stems. The pattern has also been called Dahlia. The profusion of titles is largely a result of regional preferences. Photograph courtesy of M. Finkel and Daughter, Inc.

3.26. Detail, Rose Wreath, appliquéd quilt, 1864, Newlin Township, Chester County. Made by the wives of the mill operators of Laurel Iron Works. 91" square. Cotton. The background is white; the rose and buds, red; the rose centers, yellow; and the calyxes, wreath, vine, and leaves, green. Appliquéd blocks are set on the diagonal and alternate with solid-white cotton blocks. The flowers are applied with a blanket stitch in yellow embroidery thread. The wreath fabric is applied with a blind stitch. Red cotton binding is

Stars

used with the mitered corners. Diamond pattern quilting is used across the pattern blocks and border. Four-lobed feather quilting appears in the solid-white blocks. With its two appliquéd flags and shield a reminder that this quilt was made during the height of the Civil War, the quilt is dedicated to the concept of liberty. Both the word "Liberty" and the date 1864 are embroidered in red cotton thread at the top. The piece is certainly the work of churchly quilters. In *The Romance of the Patchwork Quilt in America*, Carrie Hall calls a rose wreath with diamond and geometric-shaped leaves a "Hollyhock Wreath." Collection of Chester County Historical Society, West Chester, Pennsylvania.

NO QUILT DESIGN has been more coveted nor has more variations than the star. The Newark Museum's catalogue of quilts lists some 104 variations of the star pattern. Jeannette Lasansky's *Pieced by Mother* classifies the pattern into four major categories: the Star (figures 3.27 through 3.31), the Touching Star (figures 3.32 and 3.34), the Variable Star (figures 3.35, 3.36, 3,38, 3.39, and 3.41), and the Feathered Star (figures 3.37 and 3.40).

The Star is traditionally a single large design with even spaces between its eight points. When there are no additional designs between the points, the pattern is usually referred to as a Lone Star (figure 3.27). When the central star is surrounded by small satellite motifs, as can be seen in figures 3.28, 3.29, and 3.30, it is called by such names as Star of the East and Star of Bethlehem. The name "Rising Star," on the other hand, refers specifically to the star's graduations of one color followed by graduations of another and another. Whatever its name, the single large star design exhibits the intricate planning required for such a dramatic visual statement. A powerful, faceted, and seemingly endless explosion of points is contained only by the practical edge of the quilt or by the border of the block enclosing it. Even the word "motif" is too small to describe such a star.

Except for the Postage Stamp variation, which is made from squares, the single star is constructed completely from elongated diamonds. The extravagant visual reverberations come from the planned artistic placement of the colors and shades of fabric pieces. The practical problem of a single large diamond-constructed design is that the initial cutting and stitching of the diamonds affects the exacting symmetrical requirements of the final outer edges, which, if clumsily done, may not be discovered until it is too late to rectify. Angled sides and the bias cut of the fabric contribute to the puckering and stretching of the diamonds. The diamond-piecing technique of the single star pattern is not for beginning quilters.

The Touching, Variable, and Feathered Stars are each smaller, multiples repeating the designs which resemble their names. More often than not, these stars have their points unevenly spaced. This is particularly true for the Variable Star constructed from the Nine-Patch design. Generally, these star repeats are pieced using one of four shapes—diamonds, squares, triangles, and, more rarely, strips. Pieced repeat stars are safer to attempt than one central design, however, because a mistake in the beginning affects only one small motif.

3.27

3.28

3.29

3.27. Lone Star, pieced and appliquéd quilt, Moravian, c. 1880, Bethlehem, Lehigh County. Maker unknown. 96" x 100". Cotton. Eight different prints in red, blue, and brown are cut in diamond shapes and pieced with large white squares and triangles to form a strong single star design. The border incorporates the Delectable Mountains pattern. Collection of Moravian Museum; photograph by Ken White.

3.28. Rising Star (Morning Star), pieced quilt, Schwenkfelder, c. 1880, Montgomery County. Owned by Clarella Dresher Anders. 81" square. Cotton. Prints in three shades of four colors—yellow, red, green, and blue—were selected to create a bursting star or rising sun effect. The same radiation is echoed by the small bursting stars set into the corners. The remarkable quality of this star pattern rests with the shades of color and quality of piecing rather than with the very simple quilting design. Collection of Mr. and Mrs. Stephen Anders Palmer, Jr.; photograph by Ken White.

3.29. Star, pieced and appliquéd quilt, Schwenkfelder, c. 1850, Montgomery County. Maker unknown. 95" x 93". Cotton. The diamond-constructed star of red, blue, green, and yellow prints is pieced to light-blue corner blocks and triangular inserts set between the blocks. Reel, orange peel, and leaf patterns of red and brown are appliquéd to the blocks and triangles, keeping this large star from being a true Lone Star. The logic of having well-balanced spaces between the eight points is a quilter's distinction between the true Star shape and the Variable Star shape. In practical usage, the Variable Star tends to be a small repeat pattern. Collection of Mrs. Anne K. Heebner; photograph by Ken White.

3.30. Star (Star of Bethlehem), pieced and appliquéd quilt, Moravian, c. 1860, Bethlehem, Lehigh County. Maker unknown. 98" square. Cotton. The white quilt background is developed into a large single star by elongated diamond pieces in printed fabrics of red, brown, and shades of green, blue, and gold. The diamonds, cut from a template and pieced, form the large eight-pointed star. The spacing between the eight points, however, is not uniform as in typical large Lone or Bethlehem stars, and, conversely, the satellite stars do not have the usual imbalanced spacing typical of many small Variable Star types. Collection of Moravian Museum; photograph by Ken White.

3.31. Postage Stamp (Star), pieced quilt, Mennonite, c. 1900, Bowmansville, Lancaster County. Maker unknown. 87" x 88". Cotton. Dependent on the placement of bright and dark squares pieced in block unity, this postage stamp arrangement is recognized by Mennonite quilters as typically Mennonite. The name "Postage Stamp" comes from the shape and size of the pieces rather than from the colors as in the Rising Star. The star shape, though large and singular as in the Lone Star, has irregular spaces between the eight points, suggesting the small repeat-type Variable Stars seen in figure 3.39. Collection of Dr. and Mrs. Donald M. Herr; photograph by Ken White.

3.30

3.31

3.33

3.32

3.32. Touching Star, pieced and appliquéd quilt, c. 1900, locale unknown. Maker unknown. 78" square. Cotton. Each of the four large touching stars is composed of an eight-sided geometric center which radiates outward in strip form. The distance from the center to the outer tip of each of the eight star points requires thirteen strips and a tiny triangle. Photograph courtesy of M. Finkel and Daughter, Inc.

3.33. Touching Star (Blazing Star), pieced quilt, c. 1840, Lancaster County. Maker unknown. 90$\frac{1}{2}$" x 87$\frac{1}{2}$". Cotton. The white fabric, pieced with a blue and white dotted print, forms an inner eight-pointed, evenly spaced star design which is repeated nine times. To each star a circle of white diamonds has been pieced and then a circle of blue diamonds. The suggestion of eight more points is made with eight strategically placed blue-print diamonds. Courtesy Collection of the Heritage Center of Lancaster County.

3.34. Touching Star, pieced quilt, c. 1900, locale unknown. Maker unknown. 86" x 88". Blocks, diamonds, and borders of white are pieced to printed fabrics of red and navy blue to create each bursting sun. Four more diamond shapes are pieced to eight points, turning each sunburst into a true eight-pointed star. Collection of Robert L. Schaeffer, Jr., in Permanent Collection, Franklin and Marshall College; photograph by Ken White.

3.34

3.35. Detail, Variable Star, pieced quilt, Mennonite, c. 1880, Salford, Montgomery County. Made by Mrs. Benjamin Moyer for her daughter Annie Moyer. 91^1/$_2$" x 80^1/$_2$". Cotton. The blocks, set on point, are composed of diamond shapes with small squares for the corners of each block and four triangles to complete the geometry of a block. Each center star, though a small repeat pattern, is a true eight-pointed star, with points equally spaced and created with diamond templates instead of being made from nine patches as in figures 3.38 and 3.41. The intricate and remarkable piecing repeats are broken up and yet held together by the sashing and square separations which accentuate and enliven any repeat design. Photograph courtesy Mennonite Heritage Center.

3.36. Variable Star, pieced cradle quilt, date unknown, possibly Berks County. Maker unknown. 40" x 42". Cotton. Prints of pink and yellow cut in diamond shapes are pieced to squares and triangles of a brown print. Mennonite-type sashing in a pink print and square separations of a yellow print frame the quilt. Two techniques distinguish this star repeat from the repeats in figure 3.35—one, the choice of colors which here are all light shades against a dark background; and, two, the star block which is set here as a square rather than on point. The corners in each block are single squares. The corners in figure 3.35 are pieced of four small squares. Though this star and the one in figure 3.35 are small repeat patterns, they differ from the typical, irregularly spaced Nine-Patch Variable Star as shown in figure 3.41 by being perfectly proportioned like the Lone Star. Collection of Mr. and Mrs. Victor L. Johnson; photograph by Ken White.

3.35

3.36

3.37

3.38

3.37. Detail, Feathered Star, pieced quilt, Mennonite, dated 1858, probably Berks County. Made by Mary Loux, later Mrs. Enos Fretz Hunsberger. Cotton. The major difference between this Feathered Star and the Variable Star in figure 3.38 is the straight edge of the latter and the sawtooth-type edge of the former. Collection of Mr. and Mrs. Paul Hunsberger on loan to Mennonite Heritage Center; photograph by John W. Munro.

3.38. Variable Star, pieced quilt, Mennonite, date unknown. Bucks County. Dimensions unknown. Cotton. Collection of Mrs. Clarence D. Meyers on loan to Mennonite Heritage Center; photograph by John W. Munro.

3.39. Variable Star, pieced and appliquéd signature quilt, dated "10 Month 1846", Marple Township, Delaware County. Made by Sara Pancoast. 112" x 100". Cotton. Two illusionary designs—a star in a circle and a star in a square—are created by piecing two block patterns together, the Nine-Patch cross and the Variable Star. In the first case, no circle actually exists. In the second, there is neither star nor square. Sixty-six stamped or drawn designs and handwritten names of people of German and English descent appear on this memorial quilt to five members of the Pancoast family. Collection of Mr. and Mrs. I. G. Schorsch III; photograph by Ken White.

3.39

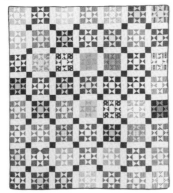

3.40. Feathered Star, pieced quilt, c. 1870, locale unknown. Maker unknown. 85" square. Cotton. The white background is ornamented with prints of red, green, and yellow, the edges of each star having their own sawtooth border. Again the stars are of the variable type—that is, there is more than one and the spaces between the points are not symmetrical. An outer sawtooth border, pointing away from the stars, frames the quilt. Collection of Robert L. Schaeffer, Jr., in Permanent Collection, Franklin and Marshall College; photograph by Ken White.

3.41. Variable Star, pieced quilt, c. 1880, locale unknown. Maker unknown. 79" x 68". Cotton. Private collection; photograph by Ken White.

The Sun or Compass

THE CIRCLE DESIGN—sometimes called Compass, Sun, Sunburst, Rising Sun, Sunflower, and Mariner's Compass—is one of the very few quilting patterns reaching back to ancient times. Varied forms of the circle were favored by churchly nineteenth-century quilters. The compass design, usually pieced, demands neatness for its well-defined points and angles. Long points were usually basted to a paper lining. A small margin was folded over the paper, and a seam was created with a whipped stitch. Each compass was set into a properly shaped muslin piece.

Examples like the complex Sunflower and Sunburst variations seen in figures 3.42, 3.44, and 3.47, with their carefully planned repeat patterns over the quilt surface, are known to contain fine quilting designs. The more simple compass design favored by Mennonites can be seen in the Moyer quilt shown in figure 3.48. Also illustrated is the Princess Feather variation seen in figure 3.45.

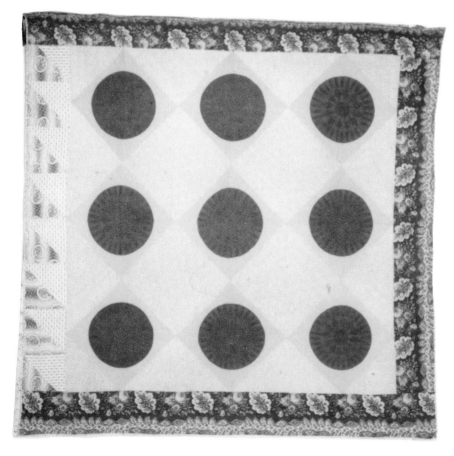

3.42

3.42. Compass (Sunflower), pieced quilt, c. 1860, locale unknown. Maker unknown. 99" x 103". Cotton. Each of nine compasses is pieced with a central circle, diamonds, and elongated triangles in two types of green print and a red print. Four sections of deep yellow are pieced around each compass to form an eighteen-inch block which is then set on point. Alternating blocks of blue and white print form this well-balanced arrangement of what is visually circles within diamonds. Three sides of the border are of interest to textile historians because they contain an early English copperplate-printed fabric. The fourth side is made from alternating triangles, one of a plain yellow and one white print and one of a blue, yellow, and white print. Private collection; photograph by Ken White.

3.43. Compass (Mariner's Compass), pieced and appliquéd quilt, Lutheran, c. 1860, Edenburg, Schuylkill County. Made by Sarah A. Heinley. 93" x 96". Cotton. The central compass is made of a green circle with orange, red, white, green, and pink geometric shapes. A circle of orange and green triangles, separated by a red diamond pattern, surrounds the white circle. Circles of similar construction and color fill the quilt. Surprisingly, it is these geometric shapes which are responsible for the round, colored rings. Sunbursts are pieced and appliquéd into the corners. A triple lily branch is worked at the bottom of the quilt with a blossom on either side. Two single-stemmed tulips ornament the outer sides. Bordering the designs are six-sided red and green shapes, making a striking inner edge. A meandering vine and leaf, a heart, and a flower are the quilting designs which accent the outer white border. Courtesy Historical Society of Berks County.

3.43

3.44. Compass (Sunburst), pieced quilt, c. 1870, locale unknown. Maker unknown. 103" x 104". Cotton. The white background is pieced with prints of red, yellow, green, gold, and blue to form the sunburst. The quilter has used a diamond template construction. The four corners contain equally balanced eight-pointed stars. Quilting in heart, flower, and leaf designs is worked on the white background. A cable-stitch design provides the border. Collection of Robert L. Schaeffer, Jr., in Permanent Collection, Franklin and Marshall College; photograph by Ken White.

3.44

3.45. Detail, Princess Feather, pieced and appliquéd quilt, c. 1885, Ephrata, Lancaster County. Maker unknown. 80" x 82". Cotton. Eight curved feathers, four in brown and four in blue-green, join together in a kind of whirling dervish arrangement on a gold background. Courtesy of the Heritage Center of Lancaster County.

3.46. Detail, Compass, appliquéd quilt, c. 1850, locale unknown. Maker unknown. 85" x 87". Cotton. The overall pattern is of large and small compasses in two colors, one of blue-green and one of orange-red. The larger compass contains three sets of a wheeling pear design. The smaller circle is made up of one rondel of orange motifs enclosed by a blue-green circle. Private collection; photograph by Ken White.

3.47. Compass (Sunburst, Rising Star), pieced and appliquéd quilt, c. 1920, Montgomery or Lancaster County. Maker unknown. 77" square. Cotton. Cut in basic diamond and triangular shapes, the tan, pink, red, light-blue, dark-blue, yellow, and gold fabrics make a beautiful radiating sun. The appliquéd pot of flowers, a natural, realistic symbol, perhaps suggesting growth under the radiating sun, contrasts with the central abstract aesthetic of this quilt and suggests a churchly quilter was probably responsible for the design. The border is placed within the quilt as a frame for the design rather than as a frame for the entire work. Collection of Robert L. Schaeffer, Jr., in Permanent Collection, Franklin and

3.46

3.47

90

Marshall College; photograph by Ken White.

3.48. Compass, pieced and appliquéd quilt, Mennonite, c. 1860, probably Berks County. Originally owned by the Earl Moyer family. Cotton. Deep red and gold elongated diamonds and circles, appliquéd on white circles, make up the compass design. Each compass is set into a brown or green square. These in turn are joined together by white sashing and red squares in typical Mennonite fashion. Most of the repeat pattern compass motifs, however, do not have such sashings and are probably neither Mennonite nor pieced. Collection of Sandra Highouse on loan to Mennonite Heritage Center; photograph by John W. Munro.

3.49. Compass (Mariner's Compass), pieced and appliquéd quilt, probably Lutheran, c. 1860, possibly Chester County. 105" x 94". Cotton, The elaborate work displayed in this remarkable quilt is produced largely by two sets of designs. The first and most prominent is the piecing design. The second is the quilting design. A third and lesser set of patterns comes from the use of appliquéd fabrics. The compasses are created out of three types of irregularly shaped geometric points, one large type cut from either a red print or a gray-green print, and one smaller type cut from a yellow print. A set of small but true diamond shapes, cut from solid light-peach fabric, fits between all the other prominent points and fades into the background. Small white triangles are set around the outer perimeter of the compass, joining all the points and subtly creating a circle with no points. Then the compass is pieced to white triangles and reel shapes, giving it the appearance of having been appliquéd onto a solid-white block. Collection of Mr. and Mrs. Jeffrey Kahn; photograph by Ken White.

3.48

3.49

91

Reels

THE REEL IS A VERSATILE SHAPE which lends itself to the circular motion of the compass as well as to the variations encountered in the use of orange peel, diamond, fleur-de-lis, snowflake, and pineapple designs. The Reel can also be the center of interlocking circles used in the construction of the Robbing Peter to Pay Paul pattern. This last illusionary motif was preferred by churchly groups, though it was occasionally employed by quilters of the Amish sect.

One of the earliest documented appliquéd Reel quilts is dated 1819. Another, probably Moravian and possibly a bridal quilt, is dated 1830. The Lutheran Reel quilt worked by a Germantown church group for its pastor and his wife, and seen in figure 1.1, is dated 1844. Later variations sometimes suggest the spokes of a wheel in the design construction. In its simplest form as a center for a circle or as part of four extended and decorated points, the Reel remains a difficult motif, its curvilinear nature ever challenging the quilter.

3.50. Caesar's Crown (Crown of Thorns), pieced and appliquéd quilt, Lutheran, c. 1876, Lehigh County. Made by Mary Brachman Kemerer. 90" square. Cotton. The white quilt blocks pieced together are appliquéd with green, yellow, and red prints to form a reel and crown. In an illusionary way the four crowns blocked together also create a negative white space resembling a white four-petaled flower. Green and white stripes line the inner and outer borders. Flower and grape design quilting is worked between the striped borders. A flower motif is stitched inside the four illusionary white petals. For another crown, which is probably also Lutheran, see the following illustration. Courtesy Kemerer Museum of Decorative Arts; photograph by Ken White.

3.50

3.51. Detail, Caesar's Crown, pieced and appliquéd quilt, dated 1849, Berks County. Maker unknown. 104" x 105". Cotton. White blocks with designs created by appliquéd prints of red and yellow alternate with white blocks which have as their design monochromatically stitched trapunto work. The appliquéd and colored blocks, which appear as crowns, dominate the quilt. The border highlighting them is an inward-pointing double-sawtooth piecing. The initials "M.S." are sewn and stuffed on two borders. Moravians often worked bridal quilts with this reel design and with the same sort of elaborate quilting stitches. Lutherans chose the same appliquéd crown for such important religious quilts as the signature quilt shown in chapter 1. But the stitched designs on this quilt—the very elaborate central eagle, hearts, stars, pineapples, grapes, roses, tulips, leaves, and corded flower stems—balance the colorful blocks and even overwhelm them when the quilt is backlighted, as in this photograph. Only then does the stitching become visible to the naked eye. Private collection; photograph by Ken White.

3.51

3.52

3.52. Reel with Oak Leaf, pieced and appliquéd quilt, Mennonite, c. 1884, locale unknown. Made by Lizzie Godshall as a wedding present. Dimensions unknown. Cotton. The appliquéd design is in one shade of chocolate brown. Each yellow square is set as a diamond and joined to every other block by green sashing with pink squares. The wide border of dark-brown printed fabric, with roses that repeat the pink shade used in the squares between the sashings, shows thoughtful preparation on the part of the quilter. The reel, though simple, seems to have been a favored design for quilts intended for special occasions. The oak leaf, the lozenge-type leaf, the orange peel, and any combination of the three have also been used with the reel design, the fleur-de-lis pattern, and other variations of these designs. Collection of Mr. and Mrs. Raymond Musselman on loan to the Mennonite Heritage Center; photograph by John W. Munro, Harleysville, Pennsylvania.

3.53. Detail, Reel with Oak Leaf and Double Irish Chain, pieced and appliquéd quilt, Mennonite, c. 1890, Souderton, Bucks County. Made by members of the Gehman family. Dimensions unknown. Small squares of solid tan, red dotted print, and green dotted print create the twin patterns of Reel and Irish Chain. The red reel, with its corresponding peels and leaves, is appliquéd to pieced green patches, while the Double Irish Chain of alternating red and tan frames and separates the reel blocks in a manner similar to the sashing shown in the previous illustration. The border is made of outward-pointing triangles in the quilt's three colors. This piece was probably meant for a cradle. Collection of Sandra Highouse on loan to the Mennonite Heritage Center; photograph by John W. Munro.

3.53

3.54. Reel with Fleur-de-lis, pieced and appliquéd quilt, c. 1860, locale unknown. Maker unknown. 44¹/₂" square. Cotton. The white printed fabric reel, with its four white fleur-de-lis pattern tips, is set to fit into the corners of a blue printed-fabric block. The appliqué is expertly done. When the reel is set more on an angle inside the block, it offers a cruciform design instead of the one here which forms an X. The blocks are both joined and visibly separated by typical Mennonite sashing and squares, the sashing being a red print which matches the wide print border. The squares are green and match a slim green binding. The backing is brown, and the quilting is of a single line design. Collection of Mr. and Mrs. Victor L. Johnson; photograph by Ken White.

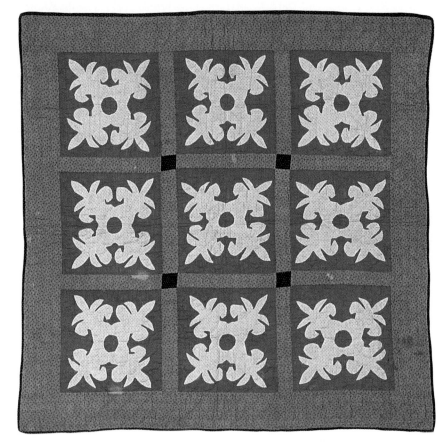

3.54

95

3.55

3.55. Reel variation, appliquéd quilt, c. 1900, locale unknown. Maker unknown. 74" square. Cotton. Fabrics of red, mustard yellow, and a print of blue are appliquéd in two basic alternating motifs–the snowflake and the rose. The two designs are unified by the fleur-de-lis pattern, central to both of them. The reel effect is explicit in the snowflake and implicit in the rose branch. Curiously, the two designs suggest two seasons, the blossoming beauty of summer and the iciness of winter. The snowflake was a motif used by Mennonite women not only on quilts but on such knitted items as mittens. Structurally, the designs are a reverse appliqué in block fashion. The four curved rose branches suggest to some quilters the pattern name Rose of Sharon. The quilting is simple and unobtrusive. Collection of Robert L. Schaeffer, Jr., in the Permanent Collection, Franklin and Marshall College; photograph by Ken White.

3.56

3.56. Reel variation, appliquéd quilt, c. 1860, locale unknown. Maker unknown. 90" x 92". Cotton. The white blocks are appliquéd with flower branches in prints of green, yellow, and red. The four straight branches, holding three opened flowers on each branch, provide a reel-like effect, as do the four smaller foliage-like extensions rising from between the branches. As Nancy Roan observes, the patterning is open, airy, and yet filled. Two types of printed fabric create the three-inch-wide interior border. A small feather quilting pattern surrounds the design. Collection of Robert L. Schaeffer, Jr., in the Permanent Collection, Franklin and Marshall College; photograph by Ken White.

3.57

3.57. Reel variation, appliquéd quilt, c. 1860, probably Lancaster County. Maker unknown. 78" x 80". Cotton. Prints of white with red and two types of green bring together yet another reel effect as pineapples seem to circle each other like the spokes of a wheel. Nine full designs are set off center nearest two of the four borders. Six half designs follow the other two borders and are joined in one corner by only a quarter of the design. And yet one hardly notices the complete asymmetry because of the conscious planning, a major attribute, according to some commentators, for calling a quilt "fancy." Though it is illusionary, a four-petaled white flower appears inside the joined pineapple foliage as part of each individual design. Collection of Robert L. Schaeffer, Jr., in the Permanent Collection, Franklin and Marshall College; photograph by Ken White.

98

Geometrics

GEOMETRIC DESIGNS, with which Pennsylvania-German sectarian quilters are very much at home, range from the simple random sewing of single small squares and triangles to the planned and rather aesthetic approach of the abstract designer. The more sophisticated the plan, the more the color shades and shadows seem to grow organically from one another. The unity of design is often no more an accident than the choice of some of the titles. For the Amish, the cornerstone, which in its German translation is synonymous with the diamond, is central to many of their quilts and central to their style of life and prayer. For other Germans in Pennsylvania and, for that matter, for most of us who depend on symbols to translate and reinforce our own lives, abstraction and abbreviation are necessities. And for some they remain defenses.

Whether drawing their names from spiritual sources (Delectable Mountains, Jacob's Ladder, Joseph's Coat, Crown of Thorns) or from the secular (Irish Chain, Bow Tie, Tumbling Blocks, Log Cabin), geometric designs are mostly pieced and are repeat patterns. Central medallion types like the Diamond and Square are usually the heavily quilted ones. But, whether in small repeats or as one central design, the allusive titles and illusionary geometry of the pieced quilt have mesmerized the contemporary world.

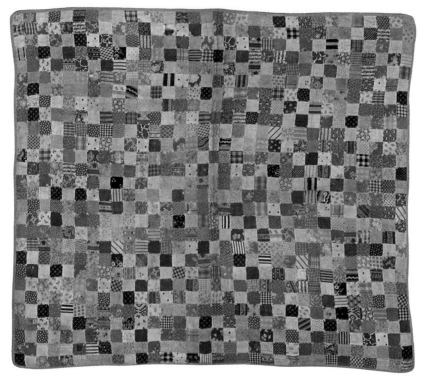

3.58

3.58. One-Patch, pieced hap or comforter, c. 1840, locale unknown. Maker unknown. 38" x 35". Cotton and wool. Many prints are used in this simple arrangement of one-inch squares. Eighteen brown, fifteen tan, eight blue, six pink, and four red prints are scattered throughout the body of the hap. The term "comforter," rather than "hap," is the regional preference in Montgomery County. Both words refer to squares and layers of cloth that are tied together rather than quilted together. Tying instead of quilting allows patches to be disassembled and wadding to be cleaned separately, as with feathers, and returned to the hap. The squares in the example shown are tied by four-ply natural-colored wool. The backing material is a red print. The edging material is a solid gold-colored fabric. Although not quilts by definition, a few haps are included in this gallery of quilts because the hap is very much a part of the Pennsylvania-German tradition of pieced bedcoverings. Private collection; photograph by Ken White.

3.59. Four-Patch, pieced hap or comforter, c. 1880, southeastern Pennsylvania. Maker unknown. 63" x 94". Cotton and wool. Four-patch blocks are interspered with nine-patch blocks. Because the smaller white and gray patches are pieced in the same direction, the four-patch color arrangement has a distinct diagonal orientation. White is not the only solid color used; a ribbed red wool and a shade of blue suiting material are also solid colors. In addition, the hap includes a myriad of brown and blue plaids, yellow and brown stripes, large red and black checks, small black and white checks, and a blue and brown floral print. Green cotton embroidery thread is used for the ties. Private collection; photograph by Ken White.

3.59

3.60. Nine-Patch, pieced and appliquéd quilt, c. 1870, locale unknown. Maker unknown. 80" x 83". Cotton. Four different shades of green printed fabric and two shades of red printed fabric have been utilized for this quilt of ninety blocks. Half the blocks are in a nine-patch design, and half are one-piece white blocks. The nine–patch blocks are pieced of green and white squares. Two small red triangles and one small red square are appliquéd at the four corners of each nine-patch to create a lily design. Across the white inner border the quilter has appliquéd pairs of large red printed fabric petals. The outer sawtooth border is a blunt variation in red fabric. The quilting designs on the nine-patch blocks range from shell to lily to square. The independent quilting pattern, the only ornament on the white blocks, is a lily. Private collection; photograph by Ken White.

3.60

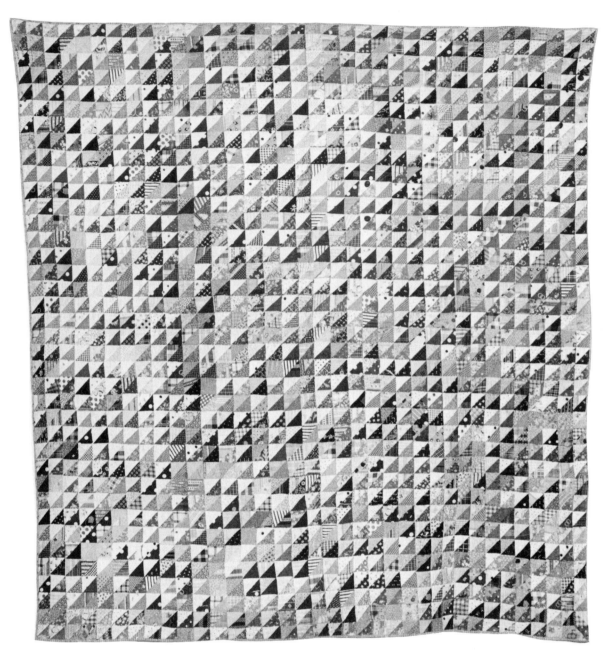

3.61

3.61. Sawtooth, pieced quilt, c. 1860, Pennsylvania. Maker unknown. 70" x 74". Cotton. Fifteen prints of blue, fifteen of red, thirteen of brown, and a few orange and tan prints have been cut into triangles, two to a small block. Like the haps illustrated in figures 3.58 and 3.59, this quilt is a document of early nineteenth-century fabrics. Like all the bedcovers made up of tiny pieces—the haps and the Postage Stamp stars in figures 2.23 and 3.31—this one evolved from great persistence and thrift. But the quilter had an eye for the power of the triangle. Her choice of a dark fabric for the triangle in the lower half of every square creates the illusion of diagonal movement across the quilt. Private collection; photograph by Ken White.

3.62. Delectable Mountains, pieced quilt, c. 1840, probably Philadelphia. Maker unknown. 68" x 80". Cotton. Rows of white with a print of Turkey red compose this geometric design of rows of Delectable Mountains. Another arrangement for these shapes is the medallion-type motif. In either case, each little mountain rises as one large triangle with little sawtooth-type triangles extending from it. It may be stretching a point to connect the triangle with the Trinity, but the pattern name's sacred quality cannot be denied since it was taken from John Bunyan's seventeenth-century allegory, *Pilgrim's Progress*, in which the religious pilgrim climbs the Delectable Mountain in his quest to find the Kingdom of Heaven. Collection of Germantown Historical Society; photograph by Ken White.

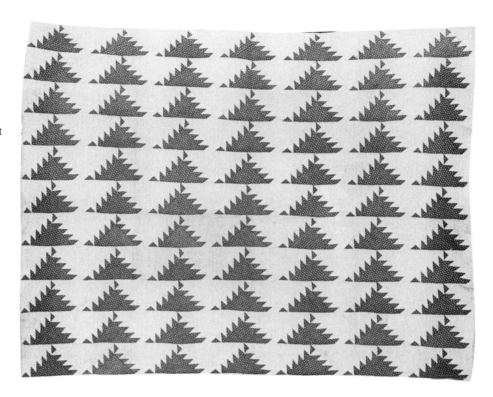

3.62

3.63. Pieced patches, Mennonite, dated 1844, southeastern Pennsylvania. Made by Harriet and Mary B. Krewson. 25" x 24". Cotton. This set of four patches is composed of four green prints, two red prints, and a lesser amount of solid white fabric. The two lily pieced blocks are each made up of nine-patches. Although it appears to the eye as if the four corner lilies are pieced to the small green printed fabric which can be seen between the points, the lilies are not pieced. The white lily is in fact just a square with the green filler fabric between the points being appliquéd and in effect creating points out of the white block. The two other large blocks have been formed by triangles of red and green fabrics pieced to the single white square, despite the illusion of green squares on red and red squares on green. The pattern of two patches of squares within diamonds and squares is referred to in *The Ladies Home Journal* for October, 1894, as "Odd Fellows March." Private collection; photograph by Ken White.

3.63

3.65

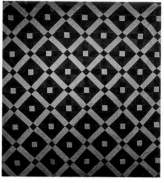

3.64

3.64. Detail, Bachelor's Puzzle, pieced quilt, date unknown, Lederach, central Montgomery County. Made by members of the Wellington Clemens family. Dimensions unknown. Cotton. Red crosses pieced with green triangles and a tan square center form a vertical and horizontal design producing a lively visual impact when set inside blocks placed on point. The verticals and horizontals, placed inside the diagonals created by the square set as a diamond, are made all the more spectacular by the tan sashing and small but deep-red squares, also set on point, which emphasize the diagonal impulse. The quilt is bordered by large green triangles, their points facing inward. This pattern was offered for sale by the Ladies' Art Company in 1898. Collection of Alan Keyser on loan to the Mennonite Heritage Center.

3.65. Nine-Patch variation, pieced quilt, c. 1840, locale unknown. Maker unknown. 90" x 99". Cotton. The blocks of nine-patch variations, created essentially from blue, brown, tan, and orange checks, white strips, and allover repeat prints, have been individually sashed and squared to conform in size to the alternating rust and white glazed copperplate print blocks. The combination of small pieced print squares, typical of Pennsylvania-German quilts, and of English copperplate landscape blocks illustrates the mixing of crafts traditions in early nineteenth-century Pennsylvania. Chester County was one area where this cross-cultural exchange was most pronounced. The quilt illustrated contains a blue print border on three sides with a single line of pattern blocks. A different blue print is used for the two corner blocks in the border which probably define the area at the foot of the bed. The quilting stitches are arranged in a diamond pattern. The quilt's edges are turned in and secured with two rows of running stitches. Collection of Chester County Historical Society, West Chester, Pennsylvania; photograph by George J. Fistrovich.

3.66. Pieced signature quilt, 1848, North Coventry, Chester County. Probably made by Rebecca Metz, Christiana and Annie Heim, and Catharine and Sarah Pennypacker. 88" x 104". Cotton. Forty-two blocks, each twelve inches square, have been created from small squares set on point in a variety of red prints interspersed with either medium- or light-blue prints. In the center of each block of thirteen squares and twelve small red filler triangles is placed a white signature square, also set on point to conform with the other squares in the block design. The signatures of ten men and twenty-five women are written in ink. The three-inch sashing is made from a green-and-black printed fabric called vermiculate. This design was popular in Berks County. The green printed border extends around all four sides. Collection of Chester County Historical Society, West Chester, Pennsylvania; photograph by George J. Fistrovich.

3.67. Ocean Waves, pieced quilt, probably Moravian, c. 1900, Bethlehem. Maker unknown. 77" x 76". Cotton. Sixteen different types of prints were used to make the triangles surrounding each of the twenty-five large brown print blocks. The border is a brown-colored flowered print. Brown triangles, set in at intervals around the inside of the border and on each corner, create visual faceting as if each large block were cut like a crystal. The alternating light and dark triangles suggest the pattern name, Ocean Waves. The backing is made in panels of black and white fabric. The quilting is simple. This quilt was in the family of Mrs. Millard Church of the Central Moravian Church. Ocean Waves, like many abstract designs, was also favored by the Amish of Pennsylvania. Courtesy Kemerer Museum of Decorative Arts; photograph by Ken White.

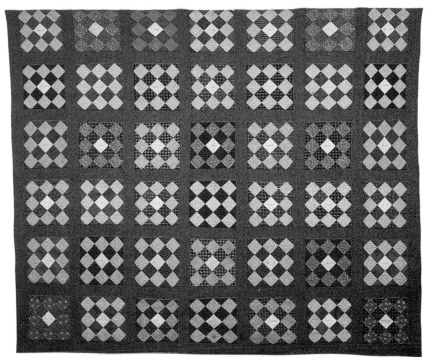

3.66

3.67

3.68

3.68. Rainbow, pieced quilt, Schwenkfelder, c. 1906, Montgomery County. Made by Emma Jane Anders. 79" x 81". Cotton. The four colors of red, green, yellow, and blue—in four shades of each—are used in the same graduated way as in the Rising Sun and Rising Star patterns. Called "Rainbow" by Schwenkfelders from Montgomery County, and "Sunshine and Shadow" by Mennonites and the Amish, this same pattern—when it is executed with no set number of color shades—is often called "Trip Around the World." The name "Sunshine and Shadow," with its suggestion of moral and spiritual meaning, links the pattern with children's emblem books of the nineteenth century; the diagonal step design, with its visual movement, both upwards and down, suggests human progress or decline. Collection of Mrs. Anne K. Heebner; photograph by Ken White.

3.69. Blocks, pieced quilt, c. 1900, locale unknown. Maker unknown. 90" square. Cotton. With four types of blue and white and red and black prints, the quilter has created the illusion of five variable star motifs within each separate block. Each block is set on point and joined to the other blocks by a wide dotted-white printed fabric sashing and dark squares. Although the sparkling illusions are contained within each block, the dark triangles, both large and small, lead the eye to the center of the quilt. A wide border of the dotted-white material acts as a closure to all the vibrating points. Cable-pattern quilting covers the border. Collection of Robert L. Schaeffer, Jr., in Permanent Collection, Franklin and Marshall College; photograph by Ken White.

3.70. Bow Tie, pieced quilt, c. 1920, locale unknown. Maker unknown. 77" square. Cotton. Prints in blue, red, pink, and white colors obviously appealed to this quilter. Striped and checked patterns are cut into small squares and variations of squares which, when pieced together, form a block enclosing a diagonal bow tie. There are 144 blocks. This rather modern motif is enclosed by a wide white-with-red print border. The quilting is very simple. Collection of Robert L. Schaeffer, Jr., in Permanent Collection, Franklin and Marshall College; photograph by Ken White.

3.69

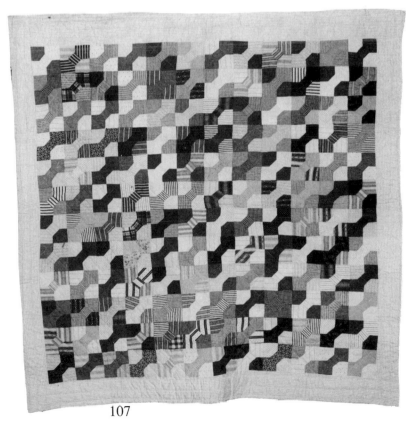

3.70

107

3.71

3.71. Double Irish Chain, pieced quilt, c. 1865, locale unknown. Maker unknown. 111" x 100". Cotton. Eleven of the prints used in this pieced bedcover are in one of many shades of brown; four are in shades of red, and three are in shades of green. Other prints are in pink, blue, and blue-green. Two appliquéd sawtooth borders create between them a third wide white border. The outer edge of the quilt is bound in blue tape. The quilter has worked quilting stitches in sun and star patterns to ornament the all-white areas. Private collection; photograph by Ken White.

3.72. Tumbling Blocks (Baby Blocks), pieced hap or comforter, c. 1900, locale unknown. Maker unknown. 67" x 72". Cotton. Nineteen brown, six blue, and four black prints are used here to develop the Tumbling Blocks design. Three different shades or prints are always needed in order to effect dimension in the blocks. The illusion in this quilt requires two diamond shapes and one square shape set together to create an elongated block. The group of blocks produces a solid wall-like mass of alternating depths. A wide print border frames the blocks. In 1907 the editors of *Hearth and Home* named this arrangement "Gwam." A diagonal step-like variation of Tumbling Blocks is given a religious connotation by the Amish who call it "Stairway to Heaven." Collection of Robert L. Schaeffer, Jr., in Permanent Collection, Franklin and Marshall College; photograph by Ken White.

3.72

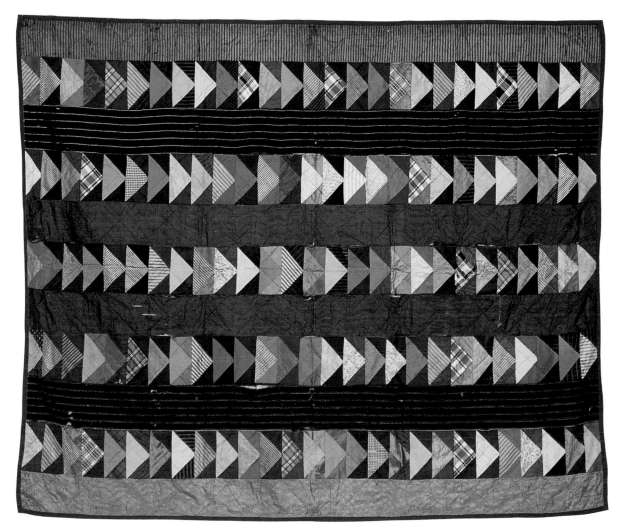

3.73. Flying Geese, pieced quilt, date unknown, locale unknown. Maker unknown. Satin and silk. Two subtly different types of rows alternate for a total of eleven rows. The first type is created from black and white checked fabric and from white striped material. The second type consists of combinations of solid-color fabrics and prints in shades of green, red, blue, yellow, pink, brown, purple, tan, and gold cut into triangles of two different sizes. Red is the accent color in the satin binding. The pattern name reflects the placement of the pieced triangular forms which are set with the third angle pointing upwards, suggesting the flight of birds The Amish of Mifflin County refer to this design as "Wild Goose Chase in Bars." Collection of Germantown Historical Society; photograph by Ken White.

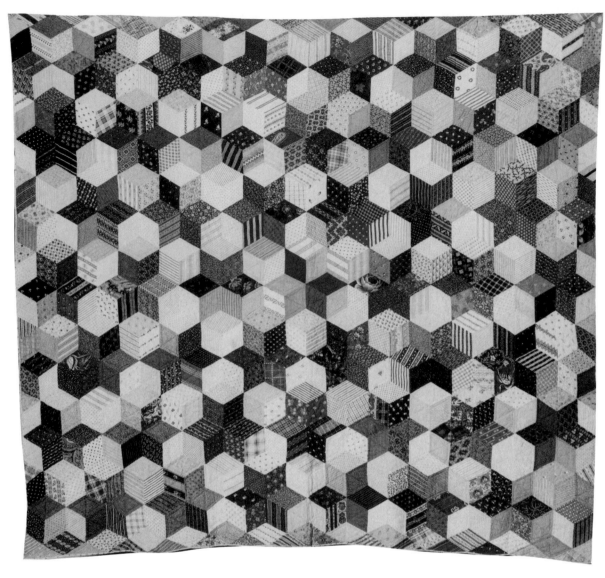

3.74

3.74. Tumbling Blocks, pieced quilt, Moravian, date unknown, Bethlehem, Lehigh County. Maker unknown. 72" x 81". Cotton. Prints of tan, brown, light and dark blues, purple, red, green, gray, yellow, and black are placed so that stars appear from the grouping of dark prints and cubes appear from the grouping of lighter ones. The arrangement, which is composed of diamond pieces as opposed to the ratio of one square to two diamonds seen in figure 3.72, produces stars which seem flat and cubes which seem dimensional. The diamond shapes here are also less long and more full than those in the previous Tumbling Blocks illustration. The light cubes, too, suggest a subtle surround for each illusionary star. The tailored, casual effect of the particular fabrics chosen for this quilt gives it a less formal and less stark reading than those Tumbling Blocks which are referred to as Columbia Star and Star Medallion. The generic title for this quilt's pattern, Tumbling Blocks, has several regional variations. In the South, according to Laura Fisher in *Quilts of Illusion*, the pattern is called Baby Blocks. Simple quilting covers the quilt illustrated. The quilt has come down in the Bishop Hamilton and Kessler families. Collection of Moravian Museum; photograph by Ken White.

3.75

3.75. Monkey Wrench (Hole in the Barn Door), pieced quilt, Mennonite, date unknown, Plumsteadville, Bucks County. Maker unknown. Dimensions unknown. Cotton. Contrasting blocks of peach and black create a stark cómposition. Visually the blocks read forward and backward across the quilt, much like the illusionary circles in the Robbing Peter to Pay Paul pattern. The edge of the quilt is created by zig-zagging black pointed lines in the Streak of Lightning design. It resembles what a dressmaker identifies as rickrack. The Monkey Wrench motif has been spotted in the German settlements of Mifflin, Juniata County, and among some of the Amish. This particular quilt came down in the family of Eli W. Meyers. Collection of Estella Keyser on loan to the Mennonite Heritage Center; photograph by John W. Munro, Harleysville, Pennsylvania.

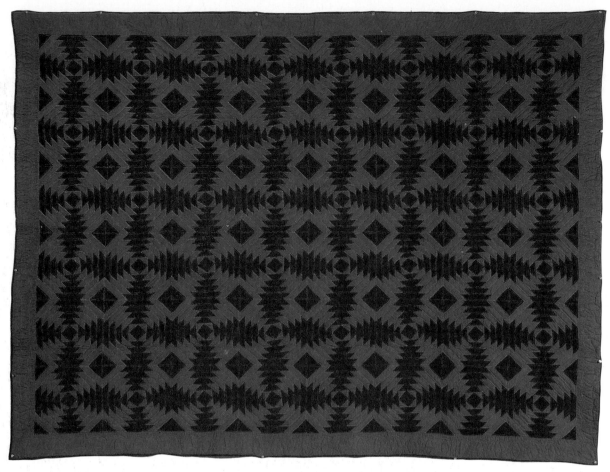

3.76

3.76. Windmill Blades or Pineapple, pieced quilt, Mennonite, date unknown, locale unknown. Maker unknown. 74" x 90" Cotton. Red and blue strips, strategically placed around a red square in a popular Log Cabin variation, create the illusion of blades if the quilt is read one way, pineapples if the quilt is read another way, and red circles around a blue reel if the quilt is read in yet a third way. A wide blue border edges and contains the quilt design. A second edging, a narrow red strip, follows the blue border. This pattern, sewn with orange and brown strips, has been found among the Schwenkfelders in Montgomery County. The Amish, too, employed this complex piecing design. Photograph courtesy of M. Finkel and Daughter, Inc.

3.77.

3.77. Windmill Blades, pieced crib quilt, Mennonite, c. 1900, locale unknown. Maker unknown. 48" x 47". Wool and cotton-wool blends. This most exuberant radiating motif is composed of blades in the center made from black and brown strips pieced around a red square set on point. Looked at another way, there are four large Log Cabin squares made up of black, brown, light blue, purple, pink, orange, white, and green strips and a few additional printed fabrics of red plaid and pink with black dotted fabric. Adding to the impact of the extraordinary neon-like radiation is a surround of magenta wool braid. Photograph courtesy Abby Aldrich Rockefeller Folk Art Center, Williamsburg, Virginia.

3.78

3.78. Log Cabin/Barn Raising variation, pieced quilt, c. 1880, Berks County. Maker unknown. 77" x 81". Cotton. The extraordinary number of small prints can be discerned separately but combine to establish the allover geometric pattern. Twenty-four of the prints are white; fourteen are brown; six are red; four are gray; and four are pink. The large, dark square-on-square design, sometimes referred to as a medallion set, is suggestive of the pointed-roof Barn Raising motif hidden in the smaller half-dark and half-light squares set on point. The color arrangement and diamond positioning of these smaller squares give the illusion of a large medallion set. The smaller pattern, too, is larger than the typical eight-inch one used in most Log Cabin designs. Dark corner blocks, created from twelve diagonal strips, ornament the corners. The backing is pieced from wide panels of brown and yellow prints which are typical of Berks County and the Lutheran and Reformed quilters who lived there. The quilter employed only brown thread in making the bedcovering, ornamented with simple quilting. Private collection; photograph by Ken White.

114

3.79. Log Cabin/Barn Raising (Perkiomen Valley variation), pieced quilt, Lutheran or Reformed, c. 1900, probably Berks County. Made by Adelaide Eck Beehn. 82" square. Cotton. This quilt is designed around three colors—red, orange, and green—and around four types of prints—plaids, stripes, flowers, and dots. The colors of red and orange function in an aesthetically sophisticated way, tying the two outer joining borders to the inside of the quilt. The warm double colors in the one-and-one-half-inch orange border and the two-inch red border pull together the red and orange squares placed every fourth square across the quilt.

Though by design and to the eye this piece looks like the typical Log Cabin strip quilt, it is indeed not a true Log Cabin type because it is not constructed in the strip manner. Instead, it is actually a Four-Patch design, made from three-inch squares (some of them pieced from triangles) which develop the alternating light and dark "Barn Raising" diamonds. Collection of Moravian Museum; photograph by Ken White.

3.80. Log Cabin/Roman Square (Basket Weave variation), pieced quilt, probably Amish, c. 1890, locale unknown. Maker unknown. 56" x 71". Silk. Pink, red, dark- and light-blue, light-green, and purple solid-color silk fabrics and a red-and-white check have been cut into strips and pieced together in such a way as to suggest the craftsmanship of weaving, a sense of dimension, and an illusion of closure. Each block is created out of eight silk strips sewn together. The outer four strips are of a dark color to effect vertical and horizontal lines interweaving. A wide dark border encloses the vertical and horizontal mesh. Collection of Robert L. Schaeffer, Jr., in Permanent Collection, Franklin and Marshall College; photograph by Ken White.

3.79

3.80

115

3.81

3.81. Bars, pieced quilt, Amish, c. 1890, Lancaster County. Maker unknown. 76" x 80". Wool. Orange and black panels are joined to black side panels. A narrow orange binding creates the simple edge. Like the Schwenkfelders, whose sensibility was a bridge between Lutheran taste and the Amish aesthetic, these Amish quilters chose black as a favorite color. Plain crosshatched quilting is used as a filler. More elaborate feather pattern quilting ornaments the large, open black background. Photograph courtesy M. Finkel and Daughter, Inc.

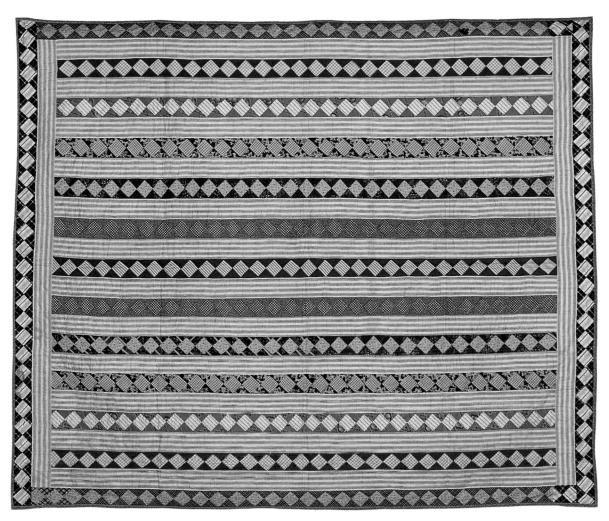

3.82

3.82. Bars with Diamonds, pieced quilt, Schwenkfelder, c. 1908, Montgomery County. Made by Emma Jane Anders Heebner for her son, Curtis. 67" x 78". Cotton. Green, blue, purple, and red fabrics have been employed in the construction of the eleven bars and the four outer bar borders of this composition. Twelve pink and white candy-stripe bars separate those decorated with diamonds and add to the horizontality of the quilt. The candy-stripe also provides a light and airy look. The edges of the four outer borders are made from a red fabric. If the bars with diamonds were turned on a diagonal, the resultant pattern could be considered a Jacob's Ladder. If the bars were ornamented with triangles instead of diamonds, as in figure 3.73, the pattern was often called Flying Geese or Wild Goose Chase. When the Amish designed Bars, they preferred the dark to the light and lighthearted sense found in this quilt. According to the owner who inherited the quilt, some of the component fabrics are at least forty years older than the actual quilt itself. Collection of Mrs. Anne K. Heebner; photograph by Ken White.

3.83

3.83. Jacob's Ladder, pieced
quilt top, date unknown, locale
unknown. Maker unknown. 78"
x 77". Cotton. White is the
predominant background color
for the "ladders," which are bars
arranged on the diagonal to
suggest upward movement. The
ladders are constructed from
printed fabrics in colors of black,
purple, tan, and maroon, the
latter color located only once in
the center of the bedcover. Each
ladder block can be looked at as
an elaborate Nine-Patch, formed
by five four-patches and four
double-triangle patches. A
double-triangle patch, always a
dark and light combination, is
set between and beside all the
four-patch squares. The latter are
made up of two dark and two
light patches. The square of
triangles and the square of
squares are exactly the same
size. The darkest fabric in each
Nine-Patch produces the illusion
of a ladder. Collection of
Germantown Historical Society;
photograph by Ken White.

3.84

3.84. Diamond in a Square,
pieced quilt, Amish, date
unknown, Lancaster County.
Maker unknown. 78" square.
Wool. Green wool is used for the
center square and the four border
panels. Blue wool is pieced to
create the triangles within the
large square as well as the four
blocks at the outer corners.
Smaller blue wool corner blocks
join the sashings of the outer red

wool square. A third set of small
blocks, done in green, joins the
sashing of the inner red
diamond. The quilting stitches
are varied. Feather wreath
quilting adorns the center green
square, which is set on point.
With it is a crosshatched pattern.
Simple diamond patterns,
formed by two diagonal-line
quilting designs, frame a four-
petaled flower stitched on the

red sashing and the four small
blue squares. Undulating feather
quilting covers the four green
side panels. This motif is
sometimes referred to by the
Amish as "Halsduch," which in
the Pennsylvania-German dialect
means "neckerchief."
Photograph courtesy M. Finkel
and Daughter, Inc.

3.85

3.85. One-Patch Diamond in a Square, pieced quilt, Amish. 78" square. Wool. The central Sunshine and Shadow type of color arrangement is done in shades of gold, red, dark green, light blue, rose, pink, and bright green. The sashing, which encloses the one-patch pattern and defines it as a diamond, is dark green and has purple squares which join it together. The triangles surrounding this diamond, which form the square background, are light blue. The blue has a sashing of rose which is joined at the corners by complementary blue squares. The four side panels of dark blue are joined by a set of large corner squares in red. Quilting in an "X" pattern is worked into each small center Sunshine and Shadow patch. A wineglass design is worked in the surrounding large light-blue triangles. A six-pointed star design fills the four small light-blue corner squares between the red sashing and also fills the even smaller purple squares joining the green sashing. Double-lined lozenge quilting covers the green sashing, and single-lined lozenge quilting appears in the rose sashing. Undulating feather pattern quilting overlies the dark-blue panels. A simple wreath design is stitched in the four red corners. Photograph courtesy M. Finkel and Daughter, Inc.

Metric Equivalents

INCHES TO MILLIMETRES AND CENTIMETRES

MM—millimetres   CM—centimetres

Inches	MM	CM	Inches	CM	Inches	CM
⅛	3	0.3	9	22.9	30	76.2
¼	6	0.6	10	25.4	31	78.7
⅜	10	1.0	11	27.9	32	81.3
½	13	1.3	12	30.5	33	83.8
⅝	16	1.6	13	33.0	34	86.4
¾	19	1.9	14	35.6	35	88.9
⅞	22	2.2	15	38.1	36	91.4
1	25	2.5	16	40.6	37	94.0
1¼	32	3.2	17	43.2	38	96.5
1½	38	3.8	18	45.7	39	99.1
1¾	44	4.4	19	48.3	40	101.6
2	51	5.1	20	50.8	41	104.1
2½	64	6.4	21	53.3	42	106.7
2	76	7.6	22	55.9	43	109.2
3½	89	8.9	23	58.4	44	111.8
4	102	10.2	24	61.0	45	114.3
4½	114	11.4	25	63.5	46	116.8
5	127	12.7	26	66.0	47	119.4
6	152	15.2	27	68.6	48	121.9
7	178	17.8	28	71.1	49	124.5
8	203	20.3	29	73.7	50	127.0

Notes to the Text

Chapter 1. QUILT PATTERNS AS PART OF HISTORY

1. The term "Reformation" refers to the Lutheran movement, "Reformed" to Zwingli and Calvin; see Roland H. Bainton, *The Reformation of the Sixteenth Century* (Boston: The Beacon Press), 95.

2. Bainton, *Reformation*, 80.

3. The original Reformation objection to medieval art and piety was at the folk or popular level where wooden images were mistaken for God; see Carl C. Christensen in the *Lutheran Quarterly Review*, Vol. XXII, No. 1, February, 1970.

4. John Joseph Stoudt, *Consider the Lilies How They Grow* (Allentown, Pa.: Schlechter's Press, 1937), 145.

5. Scott T. Swank, et al., *Arts of the Pennsylvania Germans* (New York. W. W. Norton & Company for the Henry Francis du Pont Winterthur Museum, 1983), 6-19.

6. The flower, losing its petals and dying to let seed pods live, is the perfect symbol for resurrection; see Stoudt, *Consider the Lilies*, 30. The bud was to contain a purging smell; the blossom was open and knowing; the seed pod was the union of the new life and regeneration.

7. Luther also observed that "external images, parables, and signs are good and useful: they illustrate a thing so that it can be grasped and retained." See Olov Hartman, "Art" in *The Encyclopedia of the Lutheran Church* (1965), 1:108; also see Carl C. Christensen *Art and the Reformation in Germany* (Athens: Ohio University Press, 1979), 60.

8. Christensen, *Art*, 65, 169, 170.

9. Oscar Kuhns, *The German and Swiss Settlements of Colonial Pennsylvania* (New York: Eaton & Mains, 1914), 117. Frank Sommer, librarian at the Winterthur Museum, refers to the German interest in not only astronomy, but astrology and the occult; see Sommer in Swank, *Pennsylvania Germans*, 267.

10. Kuhns, *German and Swiss*, 103.

11. Charles Garside, Jr., *Zwingli and the Arts* (New Haven: Yale University Press, 1966), 8, 9, 42 45. On Zwingli and Karlstadt also see George Williams, *The Radical Reformation* (Philadelphia: Westminster Press, 1962), 40.

12. The religious leaders Conrad Grebel, Schwenkfelder, and Socinius believed that credentials were moral and charismatic rather than regular or ordained; see Williams, *Reformation*, XXIX-XXX.

13. Bainton, *Reformation of the Sixteenth Century*, 95. Swiss Anabaptists, Moravians, and Schwenkfelders concentrated on "the Church holy" and not on "the Church catholic"; see Roland H. Bainton, *Studies in the Reformation* (Boston: Beacon Press, 1963), 47, 121-23.

14. Kuhns, *German and Swiss*, 33; also see Calvin Wall Redekop, ed., *Mennonite Identity* New York: University Press of America, 1988), 39, 84-92, and Peter Erb, *The Garden in Schwenkfelder Fraktur* (Schwenkfelder Library, unpublished).

15. Stoudt, *Consider the Lilies*, 19, 20. Stoudt was specifically referring to the alchemists, the Neo-Platonists of the Italian Renaissance, Dante, the Italian poets, the spiritualists of Francis' order, Joachim of Fiore, Hellenic mystics, and the Wisdom Literature of the Old Testament and the Song of Solomon.

16. Stoudt, *Consider the Lilies*, 23, 313.

17. Kuhns, *German and Swiss*, 149.

Chapter 2. QUILT PATTERNS AS PART OF AMERICAN HISTORY

1. Margaret R. Miles, *Images as Insight* (Boston: Beacon Press, 1985), 2.

2. Quilted fabric, created by sewing together two outer layers of material with layers of soft padding, has a practical English history of being worn under armor in the early Middle Ages; see Averil Colby, *Patchwork* (London: B. T. Batsford, Ltd., 1958), 8. The word "patch" is derived from Indian patcharies or colored calicoes with a plain field which were usually of white, red, blue, or maroon. As the *Providence Gazette* printed in 1791, "India Chintzes and Calicoes, in Patches and Pieces of the newest patterns"; see Florence Montgomery, *Textiles in America 1650–1870* (New York: W. W. Norton & Company, n.d.), 318. Jonathan Holstein believes that though both pieced and appliquéd materials have an ancient history, they became joined to the quilt in the sixteenth century through the influence of China, Persia, and India; see Holstein in Jeannette Lasansky's *In the Heart of Pennsylvania Symposium Papers* (Lewisburg, Pennsylvania: Oral Traditions Project of the Union County Historical Society, 1986), 16-19.

3. Sidney F. Ahlstrom, *A Religious History of the American People* (New Haven: Yale University Press, 1972), 232; Margaret B. Tinkcom, *Germantown and Its Founders* (Philadelphia: Germantown Historical Society, n.d.), 2.

4. Tinkcom, *Germantown*, 10.

5. William W. Sweet, *The Story of Religion in America* (New York: Harper & Row Publishers, 1930, reprinted 1975), 113.

6. Mary Beth Norton, *Liberty's Daughter* (Boston: Little, Brown and Company, 1980), 184 .

7. The radical move to the political left, separating church from state, which is so much in the American tradition, contained within it everything American humanists despised—"the elitist clan . . . a community formed by a language the world does not share. . . ." See Stanley Hauerwas, *Against the Nations* (Minneapolis: Winston Press, 1985), 11, 12, as quoted in William Placher, *Theology in Pluralism* (unpublished).

8. Kuhns, *German and Swiss*, 177, 182.

9. Ahlstrom, *Religion*, 232; Beatrice B. Garvan and Charles F, Hummel, *The Pennsylvania Germans: A Celebration of Their Arts 1683-1850* (Philadelphia: Philadelphia Museum of Art and the Henry Francis du Pont Winterthur Museum, 1982), 12; Kuhns, *German and Swiss*, 33, 34, 58, 177; Eve Wheatcroft Granick in Lasansky, *Heart of Pennsylvania*, 38.

10. Sweet, *Religion*, 109, 111.

11. Sweet, *Religion*, 112, 115.

12. Kuhns, *German and Swiss*, 215, 216.

13. Sweet, *Religion*, 258.

14. Williams, *Radical Reformation*, 822,

15. C. P. A. Walther in *Der Lutheraner* as quoted in Sweet, *Religion*, 268.

16. Ricky Clark in Lasansky, *Heart of Pennsylvania*, 71.

17. Émile Mâle, *Religious Art from the Twelfth to the Eighteenth Century* (New York : The Noonday Press , 1958 , reprinted 1972), 61 .

18. Lasansky, *Heart of Pennsylvania*, 25.

19. Lasansky, *Heart of Pennsylvania*, 89.

20. Lasansky, *Heart of Pennsylvania,* 25, 89; Clark in Lasansky, 68.

21. Mâle, *Religious Art*, 183.

22. Clark in Lasansky, *Heart of Pennsylvania*, 71.

23. Mâle, *Religious Art*, 185.

24. Nancy Cott, *The Bonds of Womanhood* (New Heaven: Yale University Press, 1977), 147.

25. Williams, *Radical Reformation*, 830, 832.

26. George Ferguson, S*igns and Symbols in Christian Art* (London: Oxford University Press, 1971), 12, 17.

27. Lutherans and Reformed frequently intermarried; see Kuhns, *German and Swiss*, 161.

28. Ferguson, *Signs*, 45; Mâle, *Religious Art*, 133-35.

29. Williams, *Radical Reformation*, XXX.

30. Williams, *Radical Reformation,* 830.

31. Kenneth A. Strand, *Reformation Bible Pictures* (Ann Arbor, Michigan: Ann Arbor Publishers, 1963).

32. John Ruth, *Mennonite Identity*, 253; *Lutheran Quarterly*, Vol. XXII, No. 1 (February, 1970), 149.

33. Lasansky, *Heart of Pennsylvania*, 19-23.

34. Margaret Miles, *Images as Insight*, 10.

Chapter 3: A GALLERY OF PENNSYLVANIA-GERMAN COUNTRY QUILTS

1. Nancy Roan and Ellen Gehret, J*ust a Quilt or Juscht en Deppich, A Folk Cultural Study . . . around the Goschenhoppen Region, 1840 1940* (Pennsylvania: Goschenhoppen Historians, Inc., 1984), 11.

2. Stephen Ferguson, *Knowing Through Seeing* (Princeton, New Jersey: Princeton University, unpublished notes, 1987).

3. Colby, *Quilting*, 4.

4. S. F. A. Caulfield and Blanche Saward, *Dictionary of Needlework* (1882) as quoted in Colby, *Quilting*, 45.

Bibliography

Ahlstrom, Sidney F. A. *Religious History of the American People*. New Haven: Yale University Press, 1972.

Arndt, Johann. *Wahren Christenthum*. Stockholm, 1723.

Aston, Margaret. *England's Iconoclasts*. Oxford: Clarendon Press, 1988.

Bainton, Roland H. *Studies in the Reformation*. Boston: Beacon Press, 1963.

——————————. *The Reformation of the Sixteenth Century*. Boston: The Beacon Press, 1952.

Christensen, Carl. *Art and the Reformation in Germany*. Athens: Ohio University Press, 1979.

——————————. *Lutheran Quarterly Review*. Vol. XXII, No. 1, February, 1970.

Clark, Ricky. "The Needlework of an American Lady/Social History in Quilts" in *In the Heart of Pennsylvania Symposium Papers,* ed. Jeannette Lasansky. Lewisburg, Pennsylvania: Oral Traditions Project of the Union County Historical Society, 1986.

Colby, Averil. *Patchwork*. London: B. T. Batsford, Ltd., 1958.

Cott, Nancy. *The Bonds of Womanhood*. New Haven: Yale University Press, 1977.

Erb, Peter. *The Garden in Schwenkfelder Fraktur*. Schwenkfelder Library, unpublished.

Ferguson, George. *Signs and Symbols in Christian Art*. London. Oxford University Press, 1971.

Garside, Charles, Jr. *Zwingli and the Arts*. New Haven: Yale University Press, 1966.

Garvan, Beatrice B. and Charles F. Hummel. *The Pennsylvania Germans: A Celebration of Their Arts 1683-1850*. Philadelphia: Philadelphia Museum of Art and the Henry Francis du Pont Winterthur Museum, 1982.

Granick, Eve Wheatcroft. "A Century of Old Order Amish Quiltmaking in Mifflin County" in *In the Heart of Pennsylvania Symposium Papers*, ed. Jeannette Lasansky. Lewisburg, Pennsylvania: Oral Traditions Project of the Union County Historical Society, 1986.

Hartman, Olov. "Art" in *The Encyclopedia of the Lutheran Church*. 1965.

Hauerwas, Stanley. *Against the Nations*. Minneapolis. Winston Press, 1985, quoted in William Placher, *Theology in Pluralism*. Unpublished .

Holstein, Jonathan. "The American Block Quilt" in *In the Heart of Pennsylvania Symposium Papers*, ed. Jeannette Lasansky. Lewisburg, Pennsylvania: Oral Traditions Project of the Union County Historical Society, 1986.

Jenner, Thomas. *The Soule's Solace*. London, 1631, reprinted by Scholars' Facsimiles, 1983.

Kuhns, Oscar. *The German and Swiss Settlements of Colonial Pennsylvania*. New York. Eaton & Mains, 1914.

Mâle, Émile. *Religious Art from the Twelfth to the Eighteenth Century*. New York: The Noonday Press, division of Farrar, Straus and Giroux, 1958.

Miles, Margaret. *Images as Insight*. Boston: Beacon Press, 1985.

Montgomery, Florence. *Textiles in America 1650-1870*. New York: W. W. Norton & Company, A Winterthur/Barra Book, n.d.

Norton, Mary Beth. *Liberty's Daughter*. Boston: Little, Brown and Company, 1980.

Redekop, Calvin Wall, ed. *Mennonite Identity*. New York: University Press of America, 1988.

Sommer, Frank H. "German Language Books, Periodicals, & Manuscripts" in *Arts of the Pennsylvania Germans*, ed. Scott T. Swank. New York: W. W. Norton & Company, 1983.

Stoudt, John Joseph. *Consider the Lilies How They Grow*. Allentown: Schlechter's Press, 1937.

Strand, Kenneth A. *Reformation Bible Pictures*. Ann Arbor, Michigan: Ann Arbor Publishers, 1963.

Sweet, William W. *The Story of Religion in America*. New York: Harper & Row Publishers, 1975.

Tinkcom, Margaret B. *Germantown and Its Founders*. Philadelphia: Germantown Historical Society, n.d.

Williams; George. *The Radical Reformation*. Philadelphia: Westminster Press, 1962.

Index